MILKA KAHN
ANNE VÉRON

Women of Honor

*Madonnas, Godmothers and
Informers in the Italian Mafia*

Translated by
James Ferguson

HURST & COMPANY, LONDON

First published in French by
Nouveau monde éditions as *Des femmes dans la mafia: Madones ou marraines?*, 2015

This English language edition first published in the United Kingdom in 2017 by
C. Hurst & Co. (Publishers) Ltd.,
41 Great Russell Street, London, WC1B 3PL
© Milka Kahn and Anne Véron, 2017
All rights reserved.
Printed in the United Kingdom by Bell & Bain Ltd, Glasgow

Distributed in the United States, Canada and Latin America by
Oxford University Press, 198 Madison Avenue, New York, NY 10016,
United States of America

A Cataloguing-in-Publication data record for this book
is available from the British Library.

ISBN: 9781849048064

This book is printed using paper from registered sustainable
and managed sources.

www.hurstpublishers.com

'Blood is washed away by blood. Honour scorned can only be avenged by death. This is the ancestral heritage passed down by the mafia, the values shared by Cosa Nostra, the 'Ndrangheta, the Camorra and the Sacra Coroba Unita.'[*]

Marika Demaria, *La scelta di Lea*, 2014

---

[*] Marika Demaria, *La scelta di Lea. Lea Garofalo, la ribellione di una donna alla 'ndrangheta* [Lea's Choice. Lea Garofalo, the rebellion of a woman in the 'Ndrangheta], Milan: Melampo, 2014.

CONTENTS

ACKNOWLEDGEMENTS

Our thanks and admiration go to all those individuals who dedicate their lives to fighting the mafias and who spared time to tell us their stories: Alessandra Dino, Maurizio De Lucia, Saverio Lodato, Leonardo Guarnotta, Vincenza Rando, Marika Demaria, Isaia Sales, Peppino Di Lorenzo and and many others. Thank you to Attilio P, the real Neapolitan *guappo*, to Floriana Auriemma for her precious assistance and Sabine Sportouch for having the idea for this book and for believing in her authors.

A & M

INTRODUCTION

'What *mafia* she's got! Isn't she *mafiusedda*?' the people of Palermo used to exclaim as they walked past a pretty girl, because in popular Sicilian the word conjured up grace, poise, sex appeal. It was only from the nineteenth century that it took on a pejorative meaning, designating the criminal organization that was to spread throughout the world.

The term 'mafia' has various possible etymological roots: it may derive from the old Tuscan word *mafia*, 'poverty', or perhaps from the Arabic *mu'afa*, meaning 'protection of the weak'. Legend has it that '*Morte Alla Francia, l'Italia Anela*' ('Death to the French is Italy's Cry') was the rallying call to arms during the Sicilians' bloody revolt of 30 March 1282 against the French occupation (the Sicilian Vespers).

It was in an official report of 1838 by the judicial authorities in Trapani, Sicily, that the mafia was first mentioned in writing in terms of a dangerous secret society, capable of using any means necessary to achieve its objectives.[1] From 1863, the criminal connotation of the word 'mafia' was further developed with the Sicilian play *I mafiusi di la Vicaria di Palermo* ('The Mafiosi of Palermo Prison') by Giuseppe Rizzotto and Gasparo Mosca. This hugely popular text was translated into both Italian and Neapolitan, thereby introducing the real sense of the term across

1

the whole of the recently unified country of Italy (1861). In the drama the character of the mafioso is that of a *camorrista*, or man of honour; in other words an individual who is part of a society in open opposition to the state, and thereby displaying courage and superiority. According to John Dickie, the British specialist in Italian history, the widespread impact of this play was the source of the myth of a mafia protecting the weak, symbolized by its members' honourable code of behaviour.[2]

Today the word 'mafia' is irremediably associated with a world of men, violence and illicit transactions, ranging from drugs to weapons via prostitution and the dumping of toxic waste. It was long thought that the wives, the mothers, the sisters and the daughters of mafiosi, wrapped in their black shawls, left blind by *omertà* (the law of silence), took no part in the criminal exploits of their men. And yet the 'woman of honour' does exist—the other, often hidden, side of the mafia.

This book analyses the place and role of women within the three principal Italian mafia organizations: Cosa Nostra in Sicily, the 'Ndrangheta in Calabria and the Camorra in Campania. Its aim is to cast light on the human dimension of these organizations, beyond the phenomenon of criminality.

The role of women within the mafia has long been totally overlooked. Silent and self-effacing, often reduced to the status of victims, they were believed to be subservient to men, marginalized in a world of domestic chores. Yet now we know that they have always played a central role in the criminal organization: as the custodians of mafia culture.

Within the mafia, men are rarely at home, with most in hiding or in prison, and hence spending little time with their children. It is the women of the family who must pass mafia culture down the generations, instilling criminal values in their children and building a heroic picture of the absent father. Similarly, when these discreet women find themselves widowed, they do not turn to conventional justice, but rather remain within the secretive world of the mafia family, urging their sons towards 'vendetta', revenge. As such, a mafia woman whose husband has been assassinated will have kept his bloodstained shirt as a gift to her son on his eighteenth birthday so that he will perpetuate the vendetta.

Women are achieving emancipation in today's wider society, and they have also managed to make advances within the mafia itself. This is by no means easy in a particularly macho milieu that sometimes resorts to honour crimes to cleanse the 'shame' caused by 'a woman's behaviour'. In this book we shall come across several women's stories: from those who play their part in the purest mafia tradition to those who attempt to rebel, and yet others who, just like men, have assumed the role of a mafia boss. What they all have in common are life stories that are tragic—and stranger than fiction.

PART ONE

WOMEN IN COSA NOSTRA

'We, the mafiosi, used to venerate women like goddesses.'

Gaspare Mutolo, former mafioso

It is known as the Mafia, but the 'men of honour' have given it the name *Cosa Nostra*, 'Our Thing'. For more than 150 years, this legendary criminal organization has ruled much of Sicily. It has succeeded in imposing its power, in infiltrating the highest echelons of the state and in earning international notoriety. Countless films and novels have contributed to surrounding the Mafia with a sinister allure. Even mafiosi themselves have been fond of such fascinating tales: Tommaso Buscetta, 'the boss of two worlds' (who lived between Sicily, the United States and South America), adored Francis Ford Coppola's *Godfather* trilogy, even if he considered the first film's final scene, in which the mafiosi kiss Michael Corleone's hand, unrealistic.[1]

Cosa Nostra is comprised of *cosche* (families) whose members are bound together more by common geographical roots than by blood. These are the basic structures that control the neighbourhood of a town, village or region. *Cosche* come together in *mandamenti*, larger organizational groupings, which elect a chief: the *capo mandamento*. He, in turn, is a member of the *cupola*, the mafia's general staff, whose members decide together what strategies to adopt and which murders to commit. Everything that happens within the Mafia must be authorized by the *cupola*. In 2007, the organization numbered more than 181 families and 5,113 members, or 'men of honour', as the mafiosi still call themselves.[2]

Thanks to this strict and hierarchical structure, Cosa Nostra has managed to impose itself throughout Sicily and even beyond. It controls the legal economy as much as its illegal counterpart and has infiltrated the island's politics and social affairs. But this is much more than an organized band of criminals: *Cosa Nostra* and its bosses lay down the law in the very homes of the membership as the system controls the mafiosi's lives and intrudes into their privacy.

The Mafia's initiation rite seals forever the fate of its members, who form a community indissoluble until death. Certain mafiosi speak of this rite as a mystical experience during which they abandon their identity and are reborn in their new persona of the man of honour.

Gaspare Mutolo,[3] a now repentant former mafioso, recalls: 'To be a mafioso meant entering a world of superior people. When you become officially affiliated, your bosses tell you that there is nobody superior to you. For this reason you're no longer allowed to invite anyone who is not in the organization to your house. You can only invite other men of honour. You know who they are because when you're introduced to one of them you're told, '*Lui è come a noi*' ('he's like us'). You can continue to greet other people, but from a distance.'

To join the mafia is thus to enter a world apart, with its own rules and traditions. It is said in Sicily that, once in the organization, the only way an individual can leave is to be carried out feet first...

Gaspare Mutolo continues:

> I officially joined the mafia in 1973. I was *combinato* [initiated], that's to say I was made to swear the oath by which you become a man of honour. They produce an image of a saint, the representative of your family pricks your finger—the one you use to pull a trigger—and blood is smeared on the saint's image, and it's burnt and passed from hand to hand, taking care not to let the fire go out. And you swear the oath, which goes: 'May I burn like this saint if I ever betray the mafia.' The first thing I was told was that a father had to be ready to strangle his own son if the latter ever went against the orders of the boss or if he upset the wife or daughters of another mafioso. For other things there were lighter punishments, but you were dirtying your soul if you tried to seduce another mafioso's family member. No saint could save someone who did that. I felt proud. I immediately headed for Palermo. You realize the prestige of being a man of honour. Your neighbourhood suddenly belongs to you. You can't believe it: 'Me, I own all this territory?!' Each of us can extort people, demand money, do what we want. And everyone looks at you with respect.

Cosa Nostra is described as a 'mono-sexual' organization in which only men are admitted into the initiation rite or *combinazione*. From cradle to grave, the organization dictates its law to its members and their families. Though women have no official place in the structure, as not one is affiliated, they nonetheless occupy a central role: that of transmitting mafia (anti-) values such as honour, revenge and *omertà*.

The family is all-important in mafia culture, as demonstrated in the confrontation during a 1993 trial between Tommaso Buscetta, the first *pentito* (repentant) mafioso, and the *capo dei capi* (godfather of godfathers), Toto Riina. Riina, known as 'the butcher of Corleone', had been accused of several hundred murders. At the moment that the judge announced Buscetta's entrance into the courtroom, Toto Riina spoke up: 'I don't talk to men who have no morality. My grandfather was widowed aged forty with five children to look after and he never started again with another woman. It was the same with my mother, a widow at thirty-six. Where we live, in Corleone, we have a moral code.'

Buscetta was a very charismatic man, but he was divorced, and for that reason he never held positions of responsibility in the organization. Calmly, he replied, 'Toto Riina accuses me of having had several woman, he who ordered the murders of my children and those close to me. He who has killed many innocents. Yes, it's true, I have slept with several women while you slept only with *your* wife but that's because you devoted all your time to Cosa Nostra.'

The Mafia are no strangers to contradiction, but behind this so-called family ethic lies another motive for their attitude towards women. Gaspare Mutolo explains: 'In the world of business there were no women, that was the rule. Women were reticent, they remained apart, silent, at home, at the market, in the kitchen, but they knew a lot of things. Their silence was important and that's the reason that they were respected ... Gaetano Badalamenti[4] used to say: "Women tolerate anything except adultery. And the vengeance of a cheated wife is terrible and unpredictable."'[5]

Yet if Toto Riina, the *capo* par excellence, seems always to have respected this rule, the same cannot be said for all 'men of honour'. A certain level of indulgence is accepted and members do not need to observe the rules to the letter (though they must, at the very least, respect their wives and not divorce them for another woman). Conversely, the rules offer no leeway for a mafia woman, as the honour and prestige of the husband is at stake, and its violation is punished with the maximum sentence: death. One example among several was the case of Rosalia Pipitone, daughter of Antonino Pipitone.[6] She was murdered in

1983, on her own father's orders, for having been unfaithful to the husband he had chosen for her.

* * *

So according to the stereotype skilfully manipulated by Cosa Nostra from its founding, women play an important but minor role, restricting themselves to the duties that are traditionally assigned to them, notably the education of children. They are also instrumental in strengthening the power of the *cosca*[7] through matrimonial strategies in which they are treated as commodities to be exchanged. 'Promises of marriage are made when the woman is still a child,' explains the informant Leonardo Messina. 'It's customary for children to grow up in the fold of Cosa Nostra since they marry among themselves. For me, that was the case with my mother, my sister and my wife.' It is common for a mafioso to ask his chief's permission to get married; it is important that he chooses his wife carefully. A mafia chief has the absolute right to a say in his men's private lives.[8]

Cosa Nostra is one of the bloodiest and most powerful organizations in the history of crime—a state within a state, a structure built on enforced consensus and fear. For many years the mafia existed without being seen; it terrorized without being talked about; it killed but it was never denounced. At the beginning of the 1970s in Palermo, everybody—inhabitants, institutions—denied its existence. No one was aware of the seriousness and the atavistic nature of the phenomenon, nor of the profound damage it was causing within civil society. When a war between rival mafiosi was raging, the local prefects at the time wrote to Rome: 'They are killing one another, and cleaning up our streets.' The Mafia, contrary to received opinion, has always wanted to avoid spilling too much blood. And not too visibly. If recourse to murder is necessary, then it prefers discreet methods such as the *lupara Bianca*,[9] which consists of disposing of the victim's body without a trace. Meanwhile, the mafia was taking care of its business, and maintaining its relations with institutions such as the Catholic Church and the political class.

To the question 'What is the mafia?', Archbishop of Palermo Ernesto Ruffini replied 'A brand of washing powder?' For him, and many others at that time, the Mafia was nothing more than a Communist invention intended to discredit the Christian Democrats, then the most powerful political party.

Stefano Bonate, a Palermo mafia boss nicknamed 'the Prince of Villagrazia', was known for his close relations with the city's high society. Mafiosi of this type were viewed with respect; it was thought that they could control what the state could not, as the latter had never really been present or functional in Sicily:[10] 'If you had something stolen, you didn't go to the police but to the neighbourhood mafia chief. You told him that your car or moped had been stolen and he would go and find it for you. There was an organization of justice in society. That was social consensus, one of the keys to mafia power. Upsets through violence had to be kept to an absolute minimum, and the people even had to be helped so that they would keep quiet and not denounce the mafiosi to the authorities. There was probably an element of bad faith in denying that the Mafia existed, and people certainly didn't want them to corrupt the whole island. But it was difficult to see their role in day-to-day life.'[11]

According to Gaspare Mutolo: 'At the time, normal people didn't show us respect so much as devotion! They loved the mafiosi, in the true sense of the word, because they weren't content with simply making money or killing. The mafioso was able to play the role of mayor, policeman and priest. If there was no justice, then the mafioso would provide it. With more expeditious methods, of course...'[12]

Efforts were made to break the wall of silence, the code of *omertà*, notably by women. Serafina Battaglia was the first, in

1967. The widow of a mafioso killed by a rival clan, she lived as a recluse and never stopped wearing her mourning dress. When her son was gunned down in turn, she decided to avenge him by denouncing his assassins to the judicial authorities. Twenty years later, Vita Rugneta also turned to the legal system to avenge her son's murder, but she eventually retracted her allegations after pressure and threats from the Mafia.

At that time, the Mafia's priority was to conduct business and become an economic force through its connections with the world of politics. During the 1950s and 1960s it managed to make a fortune in property development during the 'Sack of Palermo', when wealthy aristocratic families were selling their magnificent properties for demolition, to be replaced by apartment blocks. Hundreds of these blocks were built unregulated, some without running water or toilets. In less than twenty years, the city, an architectural jewel, had been disfigured. Thanks to inroads made in the political sphere, the Mafia created fictitious shell companies and won every bid.[13]

At the end of the 1970s the Mafia discovered another lucrative line of activity: heroin. Mutolo recalls: 'We first got rich with property speculation and then with drugs. We'd become so wealthy that we used to say that with all our money we could touch the sky.'[14]

In Palermo the Mafia produced tons of heroin with complete impunity in clandestine laboratories. The organization had no reason to fear the law: judges were corrupt, trials rigged. With its tentacles spreading, the Sicilian Mafia was becoming the richest and most powerful organized crime syndicate in the world. Yet the heroin market generated so much money that, as the stakes became too high, the mafiosi began to quarrel. In 1981, Toto Riina of the Corleone clan[15] unleashed an unprecedented war on his enemies to seize the heroin market. It would go on for two years.

The photographer Letizia Battaglia speaks of those terrible years when the Sicilian capital, with its daily killings, resembled then war-torn Beirut: 'I remember the first murder [that I photographed] ... you can't believe that this man will never get up again ... And the grief of the women and the children was unbearable ... The mothers, every time ... that immense grief when their sons were killed.'[16]

Yet the grieving women refused to condemn the murders publicly, as the Mafia does not believe in the justice system; the matter had to be solved within the organization itself—through vendetta. With their sons not yet cold in the grave, these mothers ordered bloodshed. 'Those women couldn't stand up to the murderous power of their husbands, brothers, fathers ... It was too hard,' says Battaglia. 'And then we mustn't forget that there is a strong mafia culture: women were following in their fathers' and brothers' footsteps. They'd be sitting there and the mother would look at her son ... her own flesh and blood, her child lying dead on the floor. It was like watching a Shakespearean tragedy, a piece of theatre ... but it was real! But at the same time it was as if the tragedy wasn't really deeply felt, as if they were somehow expecting it ... Even if they were weeping and howling, one sensed a profound resignation, probably because they knew the Mafia's values.'[17]

Toto Riina's bloody war against Palermo's mafioso families changed the course of history as much for the Mafia as for its women. To escape the Butcher of Corleone's violence, the first men of honour gave themselves up and broke *omertà*. Tommaso Buscetta and Salvatore Contorno, who had lost scores of family members in the war, told prosecuting magistrate Giovanni Falcone everything: who was in command, how the organization worked. For the first time, they openly revealed its name: Cosa Nostra.

It was a revolution, and their testimonies led to Italy's trial of the century: the so-called Palermo Maxi Trial of 1986, in which

475 mafiosi were held in cages in a bunker courtroom specially constructed for the occasion. The Maxi Trial also provided public insight into the role and influence of women in the Mafia. Vincenzo Buffa, an important mafioso, had had a change of heart and decided to collaborate with the authorities. The Mafia stopped at nothing to try and demolish his testimony and force the penitent to retract. This mission was to be undertaken by women, in a skilfully orchestrated piece of theatrics.

On the day of Buffa's testimony, the women took their places in the front row of the public gallery overlooking the courtroom. All the women of Buffa's family were present: his mother and sister, but also other relatives. Dolled up and coiffured, they were all wearing mink coats. When Buffa was led to the dock to be interrogated, escorted by prison officers, the fur-clad crowd went wild as the women stood up and began shouting.[18] Giuseppe Ayala, an anti-mafia prosecutor present at the hearing, recalls: 'They were shouting that he hadn't talked, and that if he had everything that he might have told them was untrue. They were screaming that he must be mad because otherwise he would never have talked. Everybody was stunned, it was very daunting.'[19]

Alfonso Giordano, president of the tribunal, adds: 'When we saw those women arrive in their fur coats, they were so enormous that it was like facing tanks. I ordered a policeman to make them leave, but nobody could stop them. I had to suspend the hearing.'[20] Buffa was also in a state of shock, unable to fathom that all the women in his family could stand against him like this. He decided to reconsider his deposition and to retract his statement.

On that day, the women of *Cosa Nostra* fulfilled their role as the guardians of the temple to perfection, recovering a lost sheep in the process.

For magistrate Maurizio De Lucia of the Direzione nazionale antimafia, women often exert a pernicious influence over those mafiosi who are tempted to collaborate with the authorities: 'It often happens that mafiosi who want to collaborate with the state change their minds after seeing their wives. Even if the men risk prison for life, the women would rather they remained inside the Mafia. If your husband doesn't collaborate, you're guaranteed the same status as before. You are still recognized as the wife of the boss and everybody will respect you. This has a big impact on the women. More than once we have missed out on a possible collaboration because of the pressure put on men in prison by their wives.'[21] Most of them clearly want to maintain their position within the Mafia, but a considerable number are simply fearful of reprisals from the organization, which would not hesitate to assassinate a family to exact revenge on a collaborator.

Mafiosi were found guilty for the first time in the Maxi Trial; all prior prosecutions had ended in acquittals. The sentences handed out were confirmed by the Court of Cassation in 1992 after six years of legal procedure.[22]

The Mafia's riposte to this perceived affront was not long in coming. Only three months after the Court of Cassation's verdict on 23 May 1992, an entire section of the motorway between Palermo and the airport was pulverized by a half-ton of explosives: Judge Falcone, his wife and five bodyguards did not stand a chance. Two months later, it was the turn of his colleague, the magistrate Paolo Borsellino, killed in a bomb blast on a central Palermo street. The explosion took place at 4.55pm that day as Borsellino walked from his mother's house and to his bullet-proof car. Ten days later it was revealed that the killers had intercepted a phone call that mentioned the visit to his mother's, and had concealed the bomb in another car. The intensity of the explosion destroyed six houses and set fire to fifty-one vehicles, while seriously injuring several people.

Italy was traumatized, and Sicilians took to the streets. The social contract had been broken and the Mafia had gone too far. Leonardo Guarnotta, a member of Falcone and Borsellino's antimafia team, recalls the events with emotion: 'I'll let you imagine the state I was in when I heard the news. I had already seen Falcone dead, his corpse laid out ... It looked like he was asleep, because he only had a little scratch on his forehead. Borsellino, on the other hand, I didn't want to see, or rather I didn't want to see what was left of him ... I preferred to remember him alive.'[23]

The devastating car bomb attack against Borsellino fifty-eight days after the murder of Falcone—outrages unprecedented in the Western world[24]—aimed to destabilize the country's institutions. The Italian state sent the army into Sicily and Toto Riina was arrested six months later. His wife and daughters would never be troubled.

Yet the Mafia was far from beaten; Bernardo Provenzano took charge until 2006, when he was succeeded by Matteo Messina Denaro. After Toto Riina's arrest, the Mafia became once again what it had always been—an organization that does business, not in conflict, but coexisting, with the state. Provenzano imposed a *pax mafiosa*, a mafioso peace, but outward public relations concealed the insidious reality:[25] the organization was as strong as ever. 'People think that if the Mafia is no longer committing murders,' explains Leonardo Guarnotta, 'it must be because it has become less evil. But it's not like that. Even if it kills less, the Mafia is still bad because it stifles the economic, political and social life of our beautiful and unfortunate island.'[26]

From the 1990s, the number of those renouncing the Mafia grew exponentially and threatened the organization's existence. Cosa Nostra then decided to bring women out into the open, and the Vincenzo Buffa episode in the 1986 Maxi Trial was systematically replayed. Each time a mafioso decided to collaborate with the authorities, women spoke out publicly to disown him. In 1993, learning that her husband Marco Favaloro was colluding with the state, Giuseppa Mandarano declared to the press: 'He is not a penitent, but a vile creature. The evening I heard the news

I got all his clothes out of the wardrobe to burn them.' In 1995, Giusy Spadaro and Angela Mariono, wives of Pasquale and Emanuele Di Filippo, two confessed mafiosi, shouted at the National Press Agency: 'We are the ex-wives of those two bastard penitents. For us they are dead.' Giusy Spadaro added: 'I told my sons that they no longer had a father, that they should disown him. I would rather he died than talked.'

Whether they intervened to distance themselves from husbands accused of betraying the organization or publicly declared themselves in favour of collaboration, the novelty was the very presence of such women, their visibility and their demand for a personal space of self-expression. Such visibility was doubtless a consequence of social change, which has witnessed women's growing self-emancipation. It also led to a reassessment of the exclusively family-centred and marginal role that mafia women had played in the past, allowing us to speak of their 'hidden centrality', to use the expression of the sociologist Alessandra Dino, an expert on the organization.

Silent and unobtrusive, the part played by women in the Mafia was long underestimated, including by the judiciary, who considered them victims of their love for their husbands. Researchers and jurists interested in the Mafia phenomenon were very slow to understand this other face of Cosa Nostra. This was arguably a form of judicial machismo, but a more likely explanation is simply passive acceptance of the stereotype, deployed by the organization itself, of a subservient woman, ignorant of her husband's activities and entirely dedicated to her role as wife and mother. If we look more closely, it is possible to identify a cultural model deeply rooted in neo-Latin society, in which the process of women's emancipation has been slower than elsewhere. This observation is particularly relevant to southern Italy, where stereotypes of women still persist today, even when confronted by a constantly evolving reality. The men of honour always maintained that women had no knowledge of the organization's activities and played no significantly active role—and the forces of law and order accepted this idea, concluding that the women were therefore not responsible from a criminal point of view. Teresa Principato, prosecutor at the Tribunal of Palermo, explains this as follows:

> The concept of *fragilitas sexus*, the weaker sex, passed down from Roman law, offered women a sort of vague and never codified protection from the law. One example of many is that of Saveria Benedetta Palazzolo, the companion of Bernardo Provenzano, who was acquitted of unlawful mafioso association despite having acquired over the years a fortune worth several hundred million lira. The magistrates ruled that, in the absence of certifiable affiliation, there was no proof that she was a full member of the Mafia.[27]

In the same vein, the outcome of Judgment No. 188/85 at the Tribunal of Palermo against Angela and Vincenza Marchesa, sisters of two Cosa Nostra killers, also exposes the stereotypes attached to the lives of mafia women. When the family house was searched for their brother, Antonino, who was on the run, the sisters hid a gun under their clothes, only surrendering it at the police station where they had been taken for questioning. Accused of illegal possession of a firearm, they were nonetheless acquitted by the tribunal on the grounds that 'it appears doubtful ... considering the role traditionally reserved for women in criminal organizations, that two individuals of the female sex could possess high-calibre weapons.' Teresa Principato adds: 'There is no doubt that the "invisibility" under which mafia women have long lived has ensured a certain impunity for the organization. Protected by cultural stereotypes, replicated at judicial level, women have continued to carry more and more weight within Cosa Nostra's criminal activities, notably in the economic and financial sphere.

Little by little, women have moved from merely delivering *pizzini* (messages) or acting as fugitives' accomplices to become real role models within Mafia families. In the 1990s they began to manage some economic aspects of the organization, collecting the *pizzo* (the protection racket payment regularly demanded of businesses), distributing funds generated by extortion, seeking contacts to facilitate bidding for public-sector contracts and even arranging murders. Some went as far as to adopt true leadership roles after the head of their family was imprisoned. Within a decade, the number of women charged with the crime of 'mafia-type association' rose from nil in 1989 to seventy-seven in 1998, with a peak of eighty-nine in 1995.[28]

In this part of the book, we encounter the stories of four women: Ninetta Bagarella, Toto Riina's wife, who embodied the pure mafia tradition; Rita Atria, who turned state witness after the Mafia murdered her father and brother; Giusy Vitale, the first woman to take on the role of 'clan boss' in the region of Partinico, near Palermo; and finally Carmela Iuculano, who chose to collaborate with the authorities so that she and her children could escape Cosa Nostra's clutches.

NINETTA BAGARELLA

WIFE OF THE 'BUTCHER OF CORLEONE'

Corleone: a name that resonates throughout the world like a curse, the curse of the Mafia. Today, Corleone is simply a small Sicilian town that is trying to forget its past, but it will forever be associated with the most bloodthirsty of all the godfathers the Mafia has ever known: Salvatore 'Toto' Riina. This thickset brute of a man unleashed a devastating war at the beginning of the 1980s that was to decimate Cosa Nostra.

'It was an extremely violent period, a time when the *Giornale di Sicilia* used to list the number of dead each day. It was an escalation of violence that led to an internal war within the Mafia, led by the families of Corleone against those of Palermo,' explains Maurizio De Lucia, prosecutor with the Direzione nazionale antimafia.[1]

Toto Riina declared war on Palermo's *capi* in order to seize power within the *cupola*, Cosa Nostra's general staff. He did not deal in half measures; one could submit to him or be eliminated. In less than two years, the police recovered more than 800 bodies on the streets of Palermo. A further 900 'men of honour' simply disappeared.[2]

On the other hand, though the *Corleonesi* numbered about seventy, they suffered no dead or wounded. 'People talk about a mafia war, but you should really see it in terms of the ethnic cleansing of an entire generation of mafiosi,' remarks Attilio Bolzoni, an anti-mafia journalist at *La Repubblica*.[3] 'At the same time, Toto Riina's men led an unprecedented attack against the Italian state. They killed journalists, prefects, policemen, magistrates, politicians, businessmen ... A real war ... That was Sicily and Palermo in the 1980s.'

Behind all this violence was a woman: Ninetta Bagarella, Toto Riina's wife. An unassuming schoolteacher with a sort of toxic beauty, some people see her as the evil genius behind her husband's power. 'An urban myth, not all that urban in truth, has it that the real head of the mafia wasn't Toto Riina, but his wife Ninetta, "the little schoolteacher" as they called her. She was his best advisor, and he did everything that his wife told him to do,' says Pino Maniaci, a Sicilian journalist.[4]

Ninetta Bagarella, christened Antonietta, was born on 30 July 1944 in Corleone, the daughter of seven generations of mafiosi.[5] She was the sister of Leoluca Bagarella, a hired killer who answered to Toto Riina[6] and was accused—among other things—of participating in the kidnapping of eleven-year-old Giuseppe Di Matteo, whose dead body was eventually dissolved in acid after 779 days of imprisonment.[7]

It was Leoluca who introduced his sister to a certain Toto Riina, a young mafia boss tipped for a glittering future. He was fourteen years older than her.[8] It was love at first sight. Ninetta retold this story in the only interview she ever gave to the press, in 1971, when she confided in the journalist Mario Francese:[9]

> You'll no doubt think badly of me because I, a teacher, fell in love with and became engaged to a man like Toto Riina ... We got to know each other in the 1950s when I was still a child. There was simply friendship between us. But I felt I loved him. Aren't I a woman, after all? Don't I

have the right to love a man and to follow nature's laws? Are you going to ask me why I chose Toto Riina, with all the crimes he is alleged to have committed? I chose him first of all because I love him and because love is blind, then because I admire him and I trust him ... I love him because I consider him to be innocent. I love him despite the age difference: I'm twenty-seven and he is forty-one...

'Not only was she Riina's wife, but she was also the sister of Leoluca Bagarella, another important mafia boss,' says assistant prosecutor Maurizio De Lucia. 'As such she was a woman who had spent all her life at the heart of the Mafia organization. But she was also quite a cultivated woman: she was a teacher at the beginning of the 1950s when she started consorting with Riina, and she wasn't some illiterate peasant as might be expected.'

Ninetta was a faithful wife who would never abandon her husband; she did not hesitate to follow him into hiding.

Arrested in 1963, Riina spent six years in prison in Palermo before being acquitted in 1969 in the southern city of Bari, on grounds of insufficient evidence. He then settled there, but the Tribunal of Palermo ordered that he be remanded into custody. Forced to return to Corleone, he was placed under house arrest, and it was from there that he escaped and went on the run for twenty-four years.[10]

In 1971 Ninetta appeared before the Palermo Tribunal, accused of complicity and of serving as a link between Toto Riina and other fugitive members of his clan. She had already had her passport confiscated and been dismissed from her post at Corleone's Sacred Heart college, in 1970.[11] The prosecutor demanded four years of house arrest in a northern town, but Ninetta managed to avoid a guilty verdict thanks to a diatribe aimed at the judges, in which she once again painted herself as a woman in love.

When Toto and Ninetta were married on 16 April 1974, he had already been a fugitive for five years. They were married in

secret by the priest Antonio Coppola at a villa between the vil-
lages of Capaci and Carini, not far from Palermo. Bernardo
Provenzano and Luciano Liggio, two important mafia bosses,
were present at the ceremony. Toto Riina would later tell Alberto
Lorusso, his cellmate: 'After our wedding we set off on our hon-
eymoon. We were near Naples for a week, then at Monte
Cassino, and then three or four days in Venice.' At this time Toto
Riina was one of the most wanted men in Italy.[12]

Four children were born of this union: Maria Concetta on
19 December 1974, Giovanni on 21 February 1976, Giuseppe on
3 May 1977, and Lucia on 11 April 1980. 'Ninetta never betrayed
her husband. For forty years she was his companion, at his side
even during his time on the run. How can you live in hiding
with an entire family? Only a woman of strong character could
have done it,' remarks Pino Maniaci.

On 15 January 1993, Toto Riina, public enemy no. 1, was
arrested with his family in a suburb of Palermo. The godfather
was imprisoned and condemned under Article 41-bis of the
Italian penal code to very restricted contact with others for the
rest of his days. Ninetta, now suddenly alone, decided to return
to her birthplace, Corleone. 'When they knew she was going
back all the national [and international] media arrived in
Corleone. She went to the police station to inform them of her
presence and when she came out again she found herself face to
face with all the journalists. She then covered her face and went
to find her car,' recalls Cosmo di Carlo, a Corleone journalist.

By returning home to Corleone, Ninetta was sending a clear
signal: even if her husband would be behind bars forever, the
Riina family was not giving up on the Mafia. Nor were the
police going to give up their pursuit of the family. In 1996, her
older son Giovanni was arrested, accused of four murders committed in 1995. A furious Ninetta wrote a letter to the prosecutor of the Italian Republic denouncing an 'unjustified' campaign
against her family.

This letter constitutes one of the most significant documents that we have concerning mafia culture. In it Ninetta presents herself as sincere, an 'exemplary' mother in every respect, writing: 'We educated our children at the cost of enormous sacrifices, giving them everything they needed. We brought them up according to the principles of respect for others and for the family. We inculcated in them the values of true institutions upon which a worthy and honest society is founded. Respect for everything and everybody, that is the credo of the Riina family.'[13]

By 'true institutions', Ninetta was referring to the Mafia rather than the state, and she takes credit for the education she gave her sons. Nevertheless, Giuseppe was to spend eight years and ten months in prison,[14] while Giovanni was sentenced to life for murder.[15] In the letter Ninetta defended her sons, in particular Giovanni, writing, 'My sons have committed only one crime: that of having wanted to respect the Fourth Commandment that says "Honour thy father and thy mother".'

In journalist Attilio Bolzoni's view, Ninetta was 'a bad mother, since she didn't protect her children and she always remained within that mafia culture'. 'She is a very arrogant woman,' confirms the photographer of the Sicilian Mafia, Letizia Battaglia. 'She has embraced mafia culture so much that she is convinced that she is in the right.'[16]

In 2008 Ninetta openly and publicly gave away her daughter Lucia in a church in Corleone. On the bride's arm was her brother Giuseppe, recently released from prison. During the ceremony the new son-in-law did not forget to pay homage to those absent, the Mafia's greatest criminals: 'We think of those who haven't been able to come today: Salvatore, Giovanni and Leoluca. We miss you terribly. When you were by our side you brought us peace and calm.'

Today Ninetta leads a quiet life in Corleone, a discreet and pious woman as mafia tradition demands. She can be seen at mass every day, and people timidly say hello to her. 'For a very long time, women—and Ninetta has been perfect in this role— have been the respectable face of mafia families,' explains Alessandra Dino, 'the ones that are shown to the rest of the world to make people think that the family is normal. These women have to show in public that they are perfect. They go to church, to public ceremonies, and are extremely gracious ... so that people can't imagine that they could live with such murderous men.'

According to Alessandra Camassa, a Sicilian magistrate, 'Mafia women are strange. If you stop to think for a moment, their men are rarely at home with them, as they're either on the run or in jail. So they spend little time with their children. Who then passes on the mafia culture? The absent father? The guardians of the criminal code are the women, who build up images of their husbands as supermen in their children's imaginations.'[17]

Ninetta has successfully avoided answering to the law all her life even though the Corleonesi's track record is the bloodiest in the history of organized crime. With her impeccable coiffure and her schoolmistress image, this woman still guards the secret of the 'Corleonesi's fortune': the hundreds of millions of Euros still sought by the Italian justice system. In 2007, the Riina family was sentenced to pay compensation and damages of €3.36 million to the family of Paolo Borsellino after an action brought against Ninetta Bagarella by the judge's widow. In the event, the sum was paid by the Fondo di Rotazione per la Solidarità alle Vittime dei Reati di Tipo Mafioso, a state solidarity fund for victims of the Mafia.[18]

In January 2009, Maria Concetta, Toto Riina and Ninetta Bagarella's older daughter, gave an interview to *La Repubblica*.[19] She called her life 'an ordeal' and complained of problems 'finding work' with the name she bears. Potential employers were 'afraid of seeing their names in the newspapers, as mafia collaborators,' she explained. But Maria Concetta declined to condemn her father, viewing him as a scapegoat. In her eyes he was not the cruel and bloodthirsty killer of children described in the press, but a father who passed down values of morality and respect. 'For me, for my husband, for my children, I wish for a normal, or nearly normal, life. I would like to work. I would like to be judged for who I am and what I do, but above all I would like my children to be considered like any other men and women in the future,' she concluded.

Lucia Riina, the couple's younger daughter, refused to change her name: 'a father remains a father. I've always felt huge admiration and love for him.'[20] From her childhood she recalled an atmosphere of 'peace and calm'. Her mother 'often talked about art history and literature', while her father, 'passionate about reading, spent his evenings reading works on the history of Sicily.' Her uncle, Leoluca Bagarella, passed on to her his 'love of painting', and Lucia Riina has since devoted herself to art.[21]

In the autumn of 2013 Ninetta went to visit her daughter Maria Concetta, who had moved with her family to Puglia. On this occasion she met the wife of Giuseppe Rogoli, one of the founders of the Sacra Corona Unita, the Puglian mafia. For Italy's Penitentiary Administration Department, this was no mere coincidence. Toto Riina shares his exercise hours in Milan's Opera prison with Alberto Lorusso, another Puglian, jailed for drug trafficking and unlawful mafia association. Might a new partnership between Cosa Nostra and the Sacra Corona Unita one day emerge?[22]

2

RITA ATRIA

THE YOUNG REBEL

Rita Atria grew up under the rule of Toto Riina, the *capo dei capi* of Cosa Nostra: the bloodiest years experienced by the Sicilian Mafia. She was born on 4 September, 1974, in Partanna, a small town of 10,000 inhabitants in the province of Trapani, a place that gained notoriety after the terrible earthquake of 1968. After the 1980s, Partanna developed from a rural district into a drug-dealing hub.[1] Two families, until then allies, declared war on each other: the Accardo and the Ingoglia clans. The open settling of scores in the street became an everyday event: there were fifteen dead in five years in this village alone. Nobody claimed responsibility for the killings, and nobody condemned them. This was daily life in a mafia village.

Rita's father, 'Don' Vito Atria, was a small-time local boss, loyal to the Accardo family. A sheep farmer, he was nicknamed *il Paciere* (the peacemaker) as he was in charge of resolving every-day conflicts: 'My father? A man loved and respected by all. He helped to settle disputes out of a sense of duty, without deriving any personal benefit from it.' This was perhaps a young girl's rather idealized vision; in reality Don Vito often sold other farmers' sheep, and it was to him that they would come for help in finding them. Of course, he could easily track down the missing animals, and their owners then had to pay him a small 'reward'. And woe betide the bad payers: their sheep would soon have their throats cut in reprisal. This was his way of imposing his power.

Rita was born on 4 September 1974, the youngest of three children: her brother, Nicola, was ten years older than her, and her sister, Annamaria, was five years older. She had a difficult childhood with a mother who had never wanted her. Pregnant, Giovanna had wanted an abortion, but Don Vito, who wanted the child, managed to see the doctor before her appointment and persuaded him to advise that an abortion would be impossible because it would be too risky for the mother. Rita never forgave her mother for the suffering endured during her childhood. Her memories are painful, so painful that in her private diary she refers to herself in the third person:

> I remember that one day Rita asked her father's permission to play with one of her dolls after her mother had strictly forbidden it. Her mother had then beaten her with a belt and forbidden her to eat for a whole day. She had had to remain standing for eighteen hours without ever sitting down or leaning against anything. Anna, her big sister, who didn't understand her mathematics homework on division, made the serious mistake of asking her mother to explain. Her mother at once accused her of not paying attention in class and having her head in the clouds, and to punish her she made her kneel down in the bathroom in front of the toilet. She threatened to beat her with a scrubbing brush if she didn't finish her homework within twenty minutes. When Anna failed to complete the work she was, as usual, beaten and had to stay kneeling the rest of the day. If she was unfortunate enough to break anything or to not finish her homework she then had to remain standing all night without saying a word. [The children] were regularly beaten, each in

their turn, and for any reason, with kitchen utensils, belts or high heel shoes. Then other punishments would follow. One might find all this horrible, but it was simply something inhuman.[2]

The more Rita endured her mother's bullying, the closer she became to her father and her brother Nicola, whom she adored. She realized that the men of the family were the only ones capable of standing up to the reign of terror imposed by her mother, and the only ones who loved her, the last born. Her father nicknamed her *picciridda*, his 'little one' in Sicilian.

Rita's was a typical mafioso family, where *omertà*, the law of silence, reigned. When a murder was committed in broad daylight in Partanna the police would search in vain for eye-witnesses. 'A shot? It's possible, but I don't know where it came from, I wasn't wearing my glasses;' 'I was reading the newspaper;' 'I was doing up my shoelaces.' Sometimes even those who were accidentally wounded had seen and heard nothing. In the evening everybody would congregate on the Piazza Garibaldi, Partanna's 'sitting room' and its only meeting place, as the town had neither a cinema nor a night club. There was no shortage of bars, though, and in the evening The Piper Club and Bar Scalia would be full. The young men with gelled hair would talk about fast cars and perform stunts on their motorbikes to impress the girls, while older men played cards.

The village's main economic resource, at least officially, was the production of wine and olives. And nobody would ever have doubted it had the war between the two main mafia clans had not broken out. For years, cooperation between the Accardo and Ingoglia families had run smoothly. Having enriched themselves with billions of lira through agricultural subsidies, the two clans had not been content with operating the *pizzo* (protection racket) and livestock theft. The former goat farmers had become business-men with international outreach. The Ingoglia family ran an agri-cultural cooperative and a business exporting drinks to clients across Europe. The Accardo family, on the other hand, felt that the future lay in drug trafficking. They then had an idea: why not use the Ingoglia clan's business contacts to export drugs rather than wine? The Ingoglia family categorically refused, not for ethical reasons but out of spite—the Accardos had just blocked the nomination of an Ingoglia clan member as boss of the Belice Valley. Faced with this refusal, the honour of the Accardo family was at stake, and this could mean only one thing: war.

Murders between members of the two clans became rife, with killings taking place in broad daylight in bars, in the street, in the fields. Often, hired killers were used: a murder cost 500,000 lira, or two million if it was more complicated to arrange. 'Some 'lucky' victims died immediately from the bullets of Smith & Wesson 0.38 calibre revolvers, while others bled to death after being shot in the genitals with a *lupara*, the traditional sawn-off shotgun of the Sicilian countryside. Some were literally cut to pieces by Kalashnikovs, to the point that their wives were unable to identify their bodies. Victims were frequently strangled, as this was 'clean' work with no blood shed and no shots fired. 'One just had to dissolve the corpse in a vat of acid afterwards,' explains Marcelle Padovani, a French journalist and specialist in Italian politics.[3]

In the end it was drugs—and hence the Accardo family—that emerged victorious: little bags of white powder would henceforth circulate in all the bars and on all the squares of Partanna.

Rita's father had not anticipated this era of change. He was vehemently opposed to drug trafficking and made no attempt to hide his views in the village. In a meeting with the Accardo family he voted against their plans. His clan would not forgive such arrogance: the laws of the mafia are immutable, and an insult is an insult. On 18 November 1985 Rita was only eleven years old when her father was murdered by his own people. The assassins, close friends, killed him out in the countryside, in the middle of his flock of sheep.[4]

RITA ATRIA: THE YOUNG REBEL

Like all mafia widows, Giovanna, Rita's mother, sought no justice from the state and refused to help the police with their inquiry. For such women death is a natural law to be accepted. Yet honour can be redeemed with blood, and this task fell to Nicola, now the only man of the family. Returning to Partanna straight from his honeymoon in Spain, he swore the oath of *vendetta*, revenge. Devastated by her father's death, Rita now devoted her affections to her brother. Inseparable, their relationship was based on tenderness and complicity. As a petty dealer working for the Mafia, he told her everything that went on in the village: the command structure, the hierarchy, the deals that were brokered—crucial information that would later prove decisive.

For six years Rita was consoled by her protective brother, and then she fell in love. His name was Calogero Cascio, a young dealer adept at extorting money from shopkeepers. The admiring Nicola thought that he was a 'success' and would 'become somebody'. Life seemed to resume its gentle rhythm despite the loss of Don Vito. In the meantime, Nicola had not lost sight of his objective: to find his father's killers.

The vendetta was never to happen. Nicola himself was murdered on 24 June 1991, before he was able to avenge his father. He too was tricked by his 'friends'. Not understanding that his father had been betrayed by men from his own clan, it was to these same men that he turned for help in finding the killers. Nicola's murderers, two hooded men, shot him down in front of his wife Piera Aiello after bursting into a restaurant kitchen where the couple were preparing pizzas, helping out a friend who was at full capacity that evening. There was a frenzy of gunfire as the killers made sure they couldn't miss their target; Nicola's body was riddled with bullet wounds, in the chest, shoulders, back. Then one of the shooters turned towards Piera, looked Nicola in the eyes and fired a final shot into his face. Needless to say, the investigation found that nobody had seen or heard anything.

Rita was distraught. At the age of sixteen her world had shattered. She had lost her father, then her brother, the two people she loved most, both betrayed and murdered by the Mafia, their own clan—a banal episode in the world of Cosa Nostra. Now only women, widows and orphans, remained in the home: Rita, her mother and her sister-in-law. There were no more men to avenge the killings.

Rita came to feel even more alone when Piera, to whom she had grown close, decided to publicly inform on the killers and all the members of her husband's clan. She vanished overnight into witness protection.[5] She was sent to a secret location with a new identity to protect her against reprisals. Thanks to her revelations, scores of mafiosi were imprisoned, but in Partanna her name was tainted; she had become an *infame*—the term used by mafia families for collaborators[6] and justice witnesses, those who betray the organization. Piera had chosen to break the law of *omertà*; anyone who did not sever ties was in danger of death. Rita's mother disowned her daughter-in-law, whom she had never liked, considering her too independent and irreverent towards the Mafia's rules; Calogero, Rita's fiancé, left her. No good comes of close connections with an *infame*.

Rita had nobody left. Those she cared most about were all gone. Suffering in the stifling village atmosphere, she too dreamed of avenging the two men in her life. But how could a young girl seek revenge, without arms? One day Rita took that unthinkable decision: to hand herself over to the law—the same law that she had always viewed so negatively. As the daughter of a mafioso, she had always believed that the police and magistrates were all corrupt and indifferent to ordinary people's lives. But now she realised that the only revenge she could exact would be the prosecution of those who killed her father and brother.

In the summer of 1991 a timid seventeen-year-old girl entered the courthouse of Sciacca, in Trapani province, and asked to make a statement. At first sceptical, the duty officer could not believe what he was recording: 'My name is Rita Atria, I am the sister of Nicola Atria, killed at Montevago on 24 June 1991. I have come to give you information on the events and circumstances surrounding the death of my brother and the assassination of my father, which occurred at Partanna in 1985. But also to provide you with more general information on the milieu which is behind such events.'[7]

The magistrate hearing her deposition was Morena Plazzi, and after only a few sentences she could see the value of Rita's testimony. The young woman knew much more than just the circumstances of her brother's death; she could name names and explain the structure of the Mafia in Partanna, providing precise details that had hitherto eluded the authorities. Morena Plazzi phoned her colleague Alessandra Camassa, prosecutor at the Marsala Tribunal, in charge of investigating Partanna's mafiosi. It was Camassa who then conducted Rita's questioning.

Having made her statement in absolute secrecy, Rita returned home. Knowing the risk she was running, she spoke to nobody. And while the appearance of a new justice witness was normally grounds for celebration, on that day the magistrates at Marsala's public prosecutor's office were both surprised and worried. It was the first time that they had encountered such a case: a minor who was asking to collaborate with the authorities. The risks had to be evaluated. Legally, she was the responsibility of her mother, who would certainly not support her decision. How, then, to help her and provide protection without her mother's consent?

Rita had hoped to collaborate without leaving home and did not change her daily routine. Each morning she would take the 7am bus to Sciacca where she was studying at the hotel management school, and once a week she would make another statement at the town's courthouse. But nothing goes unnoticed in Partanna. On the night of 20 November 1991, Rita wrote in her diary:

Tonight, at about 11.35pm, I heard someone knocking at the door. My mother and I were awake but the lights were off. The knocking wouldn't stop, so my mother went to ask who was there. A voice replied that it was Andrea and that he'd come to say hello. My mother didn't recognise the voice and asked him to leave, but he wouldn't. I immediately realised who it was: Andrea d'Anna, a boy who used to work with my father and who was with him in the fields on the day he was murdered. Andrea asked to come in again, but as my mother didn't know who he was she asked him again to go away. Eventually I heard the noise of a motor and he left in his car. Andrea hadn't been to my house for five years. What was certain was that he had come to kill me, as he has links with those close to the Accardo family. I know very well that he always carries a gun, and since he stopped working for us he's been doing their dirty work. Every morning when I take the bus I see his brother Massimo, and I suddenly realised that this had happened every day for two weeks. This morning I didn't go to school because I had to pick olives, and I think that was my lucky break. If I'd gone to school this morning I think they would have killed me ... I hope that my fears aren't founded ... Tomorrow I'll go and tell the brigadier ... I hope this isn't the last time I write in this diary.[8]

The next day, Rita packed her bag for school and, unusually, her mother walked with her to the bus stop. Yet that morning she was not going to the hotel management school but to the police station at Montevago. She would never return to Partanna. For the magistrates, there was no doubt that the nocturnal visit was a warning, that the young girl was in danger if she remained in her village. They contacted the High Commission for Anti-Mafia Affairs in Rome, and within twenty-four hours her flight to the capital was arranged. She was to live there with her sister-in-law Piera.

Rita's mother had no idea what had happened. A police officer from the Marsala court was given the difficult task of telling her where Rita had gone and obtaining her permission for Rita to be placed under police escort, yet without letting her know that her daughter had become an informant. 'After the depositions made by your daughter-in-law,' he explained on the telephone, 'we fear for your daughter's safety.' But Giovanna Atria was not easily convinced. 'What has my daughter got to do with the depositions of that *whore*?' she screamed into the phone. 'My daughter knows absolutely nothing about the Mafia. The safest place for her is with me, here in Partanna,' she added before hanging up. It was only after the officer called on her in person that, reluctantly, she gave consent for her daughter to leave.

Rita's revelations were taken extremely seriously by the magistrates, and she was soon to meet the celebrated Judge Borsellino, who had worked with Giovanni Falcone to uncover many of Cosa Nostra's secrets. Borsellino was a pivotal anti-mafia figure, both respected and feared. He read the 'Rita file' closely and soon a close relationship developed between the incorruptible magistrate and the young mafia rebel, who had trusted him from the day she first met him at the Marsala court office. He called her *picciridda*, like her father had done. He was, in fact, a sort of 'super-dad', elegant and cultivated, of a world very different from hers. But the judge emphasized what they had in common, talking to Rita about his daughters Lucia and Fiammetta, who were the same age as Rita and Piera. He asked her not to call him Your Honour, but simply 'Paolo'. Rita felt safe in his company; he was the only person not to judge her, to accept her with all her doubts and contradictions and to see her not as a mafioso's daughter but as a young woman in search of justice. She wrote to him regularly.

Slowly Rita began to grasp that the step she had taken could have a profound impact on attitudes, that her decision to collaborate went far beyond her own case and could be an example for other women who could take no more of the tears and bloodshed of mafia life. One day she wrote to the judge, 'My father was killed by the Mafia, my brother was killed by the Mafia. I don't want other fathers and brothers to be killed by the organization. But so long as you are at my side I won't be afraid to speak.'

But Rita's decision was felt by the other women of her family as a betrayal, even deeper than the treachery they had suffered when their men were murdered. The silence of *omertà* is the glue that holds the Mafia together, the bedrock of the violent and iniquitous 'mafioso order'. Her mother and sister Annamaria remained faithful to the values of Cosa Nostra, and Rita was henceforth an *infame*, the worst of insults in Sicily. In her private diary Rita wrote: 'Where I come from it is worse to talk to the law than to kill your dearest friend.'[9]

Judge Borsellino and Alessandra Camassa tried on several occasions to reconcile mother and daughter with discreet meetings organised between the two women, but the atmosphere was frosty. The mother, unyielding bearer of an ancestral tradition, would not give way: the Mafia could never be betrayed. She threatened Rita, screaming one day, 'You'll end up like your brother!' Rita was stunned: how could her mother, who had lost everything, reject her in the name of a wretched affiliation to a criminal organization? Giovanna wanted Rita to return home, but demanded as a precondition that she withdraw her testimony regarding Cosa Nostra. Rita, for her part, felt torn, writing: 'My mother is alone, she only has me, I have no right to abandon her.' Despite everything, she kept in touch with her, trying to persuade her to join her daughter in a new life under protection, but this was unthinkable—Rita's mother was a mafioso's wife, born and raised under the rules of the Mafia. She had never collaborated with the law—and never would.

Rejected by her mother and her sister, who was now living in Milan, Rita undertook alone the process of 'detoxification' from the Mafia. She was forced to abandon her codes of behaviour, break her value system, forget her vendettas and reject the mystique of the so-called men of honour. Slowly she opened her eyes and moved away from the world that had once been hers.

Alessandra Camassa, who gathered together Rita's depositions, recalled: 'Rita was a very intelligent girl, with the deep intelligence that people have when they have suffered a great deal.' At the beginning of her collaboration she was still impregnated with Cosa Nostra culture. One day in the corridors of the court building she walked passed the *pentito* (repentant) mafioso Rosario Spatola, who had just turned himself in to the authorities. He greeted her, but she looked away. When Camassa asked why she had acted like that, Rita replied indignantly, 'Signora, I am not a mafiosa and have never been, and so I can collaborate with the law. But Spatola is a mafioso, and so is a traitor, and I don't talk to traitors.'[10]

According to Camassa: 'She wanted to make her father and brother out as heroes. If I said "Your father did this or that" she would reply haughtily, "Signora, you can't understand because you're from a good family." She always said: "My father was highly respected in Partanna. When sheep were stolen all the owners would come to ask for his help." She saw that as a noble role. The magistrates had to show her the reports proving that it was her father who was stealing the sheep. She also spoke of her fiancé as an intrepid young man, even though he was a petty dealer. She painted her brother as someone who had only entered the drug-dealing world to find out about his father's killer. They were all noble souls, according to her. In reality her brother was selling drugs on behalf of the very people who had murdered their father. The contrast between the image she had of the men in her family and the truth was very cruel for Rita. For someone so strongly formed by the Mafia, who was born and brought up with its values, it was extremely difficult, not to say intolerable.' Rita was faced with a long process, each stage of which she recorded in her diary: 'First of all you have to defeat the mafia inside you before you can really fight the Mafia. The Mafia is us, and determines our evil behaviour.'

Her testimony dealt a terrible blow to Partanna's criminal network: forty-three individuals were arrested and Vincenzo
Culicchia, the Christian Democrat mayor in office for the past
thirty years, was charged with unlawful mafia association and conspiracy to murder. In the village, meanwhile, Rita was despised by
everyone as 'the girl who betrayed her family' or 'the narc'. Like all
state witnesses, Rita was forced to leave Sicily and start a new life
elsewhere, with a new identity and under police protection.

In Rome she and Piera had five happy months despite the
constraints and complications of life under witness protection.
Permission was needed for any and every outing, and just as the
women were starting to feel at home in a particular neighbourhood they would be moved. Rita was not allowed to go to college, which was deemed too dangerous, and was restricted to a
correspondence course with the Sicilian hotel management
school. She did, sometimes manage to escape the protection
system and walk the streets of Rome. She seemed to rediscover
her appetite for life, even falling in love with a boy of her age,
Gabriele, whom she met during an escapade to St Peter's Basilica.
The young couple made plans to live together, but Gabriele was
doing his military service and was stationed in Albania for several
months. They were never to see each other again.[11]

At this time the Sicilian Mafia, under the orders of Toto
Riina, 'Butcher of Corleone', was waging its pitiless war against
the Italian state. On 23 May 1992 at 5.58pm, the National
Institute of Geophysics and Volcanology station at Mount Erice
recorded an alarming seismic event some 50 kilometres away.
This was no earthquake, but the shockwave produced by the
phenomenal explosion on the motorway that killed Judge
Giovanni Falcone, his wife and three bodyguards. Less than two
months later, it was Paolo Borsellino's turn. The next day's headlines read, 'And now Borsellino!', 'The summer of massacres',
'Italy dishonoured'. The country was in mourning. With the

deaths of these two figureheads, hope for 'another Italy' seemed to disappear.

It was Piera's father who broke the news to the two young women on the phone. Rita was stunned. Her protector, the only person she could trust, had just been assassinated. Fate, it seemed, was relentless: all the men she loved had been killed by the Mafia. She refused to watch the news that evening as she paced around the apartment, noting in her diary before she went to bed: 'Now that Borsellino is dead, nobody can understand the void that he has left in my life. Everybody is afraid, but the only thing I'm afraid of is that the Mafia state will win and that poor stupid magistrates tilting at windmills will be killed. Borsellino, you died for what you believe in. But without you, I'm dead too.'

In the following days Rita fell into a deep depression. She said that she wanted to live on her own, and the protection agency found her a small apartment. A week after the attack on Borsellino, on 26 July 1992, Rita spent the night there for the first time. Piera had gone to Sicily for the weekend to see her parents. Rita, who was meant to go with her, chose in the end to stay behind. She decided to unpack her possessions that day—but the cardboard boxes would never be opened.

Rita threw herself from the seventh floor of the building. On the wall she had pencilled in large letters: 'I love you, I can't live without you. Everything is over, goodbye.' Her collaboration with the justice system had only lasted nine months.

Nobody truly knows what happened. Was it premeditated? According to Piera, Rita was lucid at the time of the suicide. For Alessandra Camassa, 'her entire history can be seen to vindicate her act. A father murdered, a brother murdered, a mother and sister who reject her, and Borsellino dead. I think the judge's murder made her believe that her sacrifice had been in vain, that what she had done was pointless.'

Police investigations in the apartment and an autopsy excluded the involvement of another party, yet some wondered whether

Rita had been killed. Her murder could have been dressed up as a suicide to hide the failings of the witness protection system, which, if made public, could discourage mafiosi from turning themselves in during this period of extreme tension between the organization and the state. Many discount this theory, but there are also some who are critical of the individuals in charge of Rita's protection, insisting that they should not have left her alone in a moment of crisis and showing symptoms of depression after Borsellino's death.

Yet the drama of this young woman's life was not yet over. The Mafia never forgives those who betray it—even when dead. Rita was buried in her hometown of Partanna on 31 July 1992. As a security measure neither Piera nor the investigating magistrates who had worked with Rita were present at the funeral. Not a single villager was present, out of conviction or through fear of mafia reprisals. Nor did her mother attend; was she afraid or had she truly disowned her daughter? A journalist who asked the new mayor's wife if she would go to the funeral was told that she was unable to attend as she had to go to the beach. The priest, Don Gaetano, was clear where he stood: 'I'm here on the orders of my superiors. She was a suicide. She has no right to a mass.' Yet a week earlier a mass had been said for Raul Gardini, a prominent Italian businessman who had also committed suicide. As a final insult, the priest added, 'Rita had a lot of honest people arrested in this village...'

On the other hand, Rita's tragic destiny had moved that part of Sicily that wants to free itself from the Mafia's hold. A group of women in Palermo decided to pay her the tribute she deserved. A delegation was formed to attend the funeral by Letizia Battaglia, the photographer and activist, Michela Buscemi, a state witness like Rita, and the anti-mafia militant Anna Puglisi, together with other women from the Association of Sicilian Women Against the Mafia[12] and the committee of 'Women of the Fast'.[13] A dignified cortege of many anonymous mourners accompanied Rita to her final resting place. Letizia Battaglia recalls: 'It was very painful, and sad. There was just this coffin and nothing else. It was so simple compared to the magnificent rich wood coffins of mafiosi. It looked shabby.'[14]

Telegrams and postcards began to pour in from all over Italy. On one of the cards, sent from Turin and addressed to 'Rita Atria, Partanna Cemetery', was written: 'Rita, you issued a warning to many. You supported hands that were growing weak. You live in the hearts of all honest Italians.'

Several months after Rita's funeral, on 2 November, All Souls' Day, her mother finally went to her grave, not to pay her respects, but with a hammer, to destroy her daughter's grave marker.[15] This tablet carried a text chosen by Piera, the hated daughter-in-law, which immortalized Rita's betrayal in marble: 'Truth lives.' Giovanna had received authorization to have her daughter's remains moved from the Aiello family tomb—where Rita, as she had wished, lay beside her brother Nicola—to the Atria tomb. Today Rita lies alongside her father, but on the headstone her name does not appear. There is simply a very old photo of her, in which she is unrecognizable. Why would Rita's mother not want her name on the gravestone? To villagers she would reply, 'I know it's my daughter, I don't need it in writing!'

Nearly a year later, on 12 October 1993, Giovanna Atria was given a suspended sentence of two months and twenty days in prison for the profanation of a grave. As the verdict was read out she remained silent—as always.[16]

The mafia, as is its way, never forgives, and pursues the dead right to their graves. Rita's mother still lives in Partanna. In all these years, she has never encountered any problems with the organization, because she has not once honoured the memory of her daughter, the *infame*.

3

GIUSY VITALE

THE FIRST 'GODMOTHER' OF COSA NOSTRA

After the murders of Judges Falcone and Borsellino in 1992, a real shockwave hit the country as the Italian state finally became aware of the mafia's destructive power and decided to respond with force: war was declared and the military deployed in Sicily. The objective was clear: to force this seditious land to submit to Rome.

On 15 April 1993, the 'godfather of godfathers', Toto Riina, was arrested in Palermo after nearly twenty-five years on the run. His capture led to hundreds of arrests among mafiosi, and worse, many of them began collaborating with the judiciary during their detention. Struck at its very core, in order to survive the organization needed people who could be trusted, who knew the rules of the Mafia. And who remained to take over and run the business? Women.

Partinico, a little town of 32,000 inhabitants some 40 kilometres from Palermo, was no exception to the rule. It was there that Vitale clan ruled, one of the most violent families of Cosa Nostra. Drug trafficking, corrupt construction bidding, extortion—no kind of criminal activity was beyond their reach. 'At that time

Partinico felt like Beirut. People who didn't pay up in the racket had their cars burnt. Businesses that didn't give in and pay a tax to 'friends' couldn't carry on. It was a region devastated by the hold of the Mafia,' recalls the journalist Pino Maniaci.

On 14 April 1998, Vito Vitale, the local boss and a faithful ally of Toto Riina, was arrested and incarcerated, soon to be joined by the top ranks of his clan, which was now effectively decapitated. In order not to lose their influence in the area the Vitale brothers decided to appoint a woman as regional head, their sister Giusy. It was an unprecedented decision in the history of Cosa Nostra as women are not formally affiliated and cannot, at least in principle, take leadership roles. But the Mafia is nothing if not pragmatic, and it needed to adapt if it was to survive.

Later, when questioned by police, Giusy was to declare:

I learned by watching. There is no specific initiation ceremony for women; all their life is an initiation ceremony if there are mafiosi in their home. They have to understand without asking questions, be available to help without knowing why, put together little bits of information like pieces of a jigsaw. I saw my brothers Nardo and Vito always on the move. Nothing stopped them, not jail and not being on the run. And it didn't bother me either, even when they ended up in prison, quite the opposite...

It was into this climate of violence that Giusy Vitale was born on 25 February 1972. She was the youngest of five children: Leonardo, called 'Nardo', was born in 1955; Michele in 1957; Vito in 1959; and Antonina, or 'Nina', in 1962. Her mother was thirty-nine and her father forty-nine, and as she recalled in her autobiography: 'When I was little it felt like my parents were my grandparents. They seemed old and tired to me. My brothers, on the other hand, were full of energy and I worshipped them. I wanted to be with them, I followed them everywhere, even when they were meeting girls.' She continues: 'My brothers taught me everything and protected me. If something happened to me there was always Nardo, Michele and Vito to take care of me. And they really did in their own way, with tenderness but also sometimes with violence.'[1] The Vitale brothers did indeed have an extremely violent side, and nobody could escape it, not their sisters or their mother, nor even their father, who on several occasions was the victim of their brutality.

Giusy's father, Giovanni, was a farmer working in the fields of Baronia, where he raised cattle, sheep and horses. He did not belong to Cosa Nostra. 'He knew the organization, but feared it, like all honest fathers who bring up children in Sicily. He wanted his sons to stay away from the Mafia because he knew that it's a death trap that will close on you, sooner or later. That's why he always took Nardo, Michele and Vito with him to the country-side, hoping that the tough but healthy life there would keep them safe from the temptations of Cosa Nostra,' explains Giusy:

> As far back as I can remember, my memory of my brothers is connected to prison, police stations and police officers. It was always my mother who took care of Nardo, Michele and Vito when they finished prison, it was her that ran to the lawyers, who looked after all the legal aspects. And she did it all without ever complaining. But she suffered in silence and I could feel it. I wanted to do something for my brothers too, but especially for my mother. So I became her shadow. I followed her every-where, and from the age of six I started going with her to police sta-tions, to lawyers' offices and to prisons. Going to school and dealing with my brothers' legal worries: that sums up my whole childhood and adolescence.

Giusy's brothers started their delinquent careers early on. They started with petty crime—driving without a licence, counterfeit wine—but everything changed when their father Giovanni was unjustly arrested and imprisoned at the end of the 1960s. He was accused of involvement in a *fuitina* ('little escape' in Sicilian),[2] a form of abduction that was practised in Sicily in order to com-promise a young woman and force her to marry. Young people in love would often choose to elope for their sexual activity to be explicit (or presumed), and their parents, faced with a fait accompli, had no choice but to consent to a 'reparatory marriage'.

In fact, it was Giusy's uncle who had organized the young woman's abduction, but the court concluded that Giovanni was involved. When, four years later, she revealed what had really happened, Giovanni Vitale was released. During those four years Giusy's brothers raged, lashing out at everything and everyone, and particularly at the state and the justice system. This was a delicate period of their adolescence, just the moment when they needed a masculine role model. According to Giusy:

> When my father came out of prison my brothers had already become men and had learnt to get by on their own. Nardo was already nineteen and no longer listened to my father. All three of them started to rebel and to defy his authority, going so far as to hit him. In between their stints in jail they were in contact with members of Cosa Nostra. In particular they got to know Antonino Geraci, known as Nenè, who was the boss of Partinico in the late 1960s and an ally of Toto Riina. Mafia life held a much greater fascination for them than a life of agricultural work.

'The atmosphere at home was always tense, frightening, we almost never laughed,' she continues. 'We women stayed at home waiting for our men, not knowing what mood they would be in when they returned. And there would be trouble if things weren't done as they had ordered. Nina, who was older than me and the best behaved, was their punchbag: they hit her for no reason. One day Michele attacked her because she had put on a bit of mascara. It wasn't enough for them to mistreat us. They wanted to control our lives.'

When Nina was nineteen she started secretly seeing Piero, a young baker. As it was too dangerous to meet in public, they had to make do with talking on the phone or exchanging little messages when Piero was on his rounds near the Vitale home. Giusy's mother knew about the relationship but was careful not to men-tion it to her sons. Yet Vito somehow found out, and one day, when he saw Piero in the village, mad with rage, he leapt at him, punching and kicking, leaving him unconscious in a pool of blood. But that wasn't enough for Vito. He then went to the house that Leonardo was planning to move into with his wife after their wedding. Nina was already there, helping to prepare the house for the presentation of the bride's trousseau, a Sicilian tradition. The two brothers beat her up too, breaking her finger as she tried to protect herself. They then moved on to the family home and attacked their mother for concealing the relationship, breaking her nose. They forced Nina to stand, humiliated and bruised, her eyes still red, in front of the guests who had come to the trousseau ceremony so that everybody could see what had happened to her.

Giusy didn't escape this treatment either. One day when arguing with Vito after dinner, she refused to finish her soup. When he ordered her to finish and she again refused he seized her head and forced it into the soup plate until she could not breathe. To this day, Giusy is half deaf in one ear: a slap from Vito burst her eardrum.

Yet despite all this, Giusy had more respect for her brothers than for her parents, considering them as her role models, her heroes. 'I only existed if my brothers let me exist: I wanted to attract their attention, read in their eyes that I was important to them. I was the youngest in the family, and above all I was a girl: maybe that was why I was endlessly trying to prove that I was somebody too.' Nonetheless, Giusy was under no illusions about their personalities: 'My brothers also had their dark side. The slightest thing could make them violent. Nardo had done boxing and he was never the last to get into a fight. He was sure of himself, he had the aura of a leader. He was probably the boss among my brothers. I once saw him punch a man hard in the face because he'd accidentally bumped into him in the street.'[3]

Vito was hardly any better. One day when he was cleaning out a barn a cow butted him with its horn and pushed him against the wall. He was stunned for a couple of minutes but when he got to his feet I could see his face distorted with rage. He picked up a spade and started hitting the cow about the head with it. Then he aimed a single punch between the cow's horns and it dropped down dead. After, I would often heard him boasting about that story ... He would say: 'Man or beast, woe betide anyone who touches a Vitale!'

Michele, the youngest brother, was the least violent of the three and never wanted to join Cosa Nostra. To escape its influence he decided to move out of Sicily to Bologna, where he started a construction business with a friend from Partinico who was already there. It rapidly became a success, and although Leonardo and Vito frequently visited in order to persuade him to return to Sicily, Michele stood firm, staying in Emilia-Romagna and founding a transport business. But being a Vitale is not without its risks, and his origins eventually caught up with him when he was unjustly accused of drug dealing and stealing sports cars, arrested and jailed. Two years later he was finally proven innocent and released but he was now the victim of his bad reputation in Bologna and preferred to return to Sicily. Once there he explained to his brothers that he wanted no more problems with the authorities and that he wanted nothing to do with the bad company they kept. He started a poultry farm and took over the family's agricultural land.

Giusy was growing up and soon felt trapped in a life dictated by her brothers. 'I wasn't like other girls of my age, I didn't have girlfriends and couldn't go into town ... I think I had meant a lot to my brothers, but growing older, their love faded and I started to feel stifled.' She looked for a way out and found it at the age of seventeen when she encountered Angelo. They had been at primary school together, and Angelo was working for Giusy's brother Michele, in charge of electrical works at the poultry farm at Santa Lucia di Sicilia. He would sometimes come to the house to talk to Michele, and one day, when her brother was away, he asked to speak alone with Giusy. She refused, and when he came to the house again she did everything she could to avoid being alone with him—until the day she came face to face with him in the family fields at Baronia. He told her that he 'wanted to get together' with her; she asked him for a few days to consider it. One day, as she was going to the shops she saw Angelo in his car. He wound down the window and asked, 'So?' She replied, 'Yes, let's get together.'

Of course Giusy said nothing of this relationship to her brothers, and only her parents knew about it. On her eighteenth birthday Angelo sent her a huge bouquet of eighteen red roses, and when Leonardo asked her who they were from she was afraid to admit the truth and said they were a gift from a girlfriend. The Vitale brothers were not so easily duped and soon discovered the sender's true identity. They then ordered their sister, father and mother to join them at the Baronia smallholding, where they started insulting Giusy with vulgar jokes. When she tried to speak up they became furious, moving towards her with 'that glint of madness that they sometimes had in their eyes', but Giusy's father stood in the way. The two brothers then turned on him, even angrier, since he had known and done nothing. 'What do you want, you good-for-nothing? You're the one who should have killed her and now it's up to us to do what you didn't!' they screamed. It was Giusy's father who ought to have beaten her, they insisted, to bring her back on the straight and narrow and stop her dishonouring the family. Blows rained down on Giusy and her father, while her terrified mother tried to intervene, only to be beaten mercilessly in turn. The brothers made them get up and drag themselves to a nearby well. Grabbing them by their heads, they forced them to look down the well shaft. 'That's where you'll all end up,' they said menacingly before walking away.

Giusy was not to be intimidated. One day, when her brothers had gone out, she decided to go to the beach with Angelo. She had not reckoned on Leonardo arriving back earlier than expected, and that he would be looking for her everywhere. When she came home he was waiting for her on the doorstep with wire to strangle her. Trapped, she now knew that the Baronia episode was just a warning and that Leonardo was capable of killing her. Then and there she decided to run away with Angelo, a *fuitina*. She was eloping less out of love than in an attempt to appease her brothers, believing that going away for a time and formalizing her relationship with Angelo would improve things.

The young woman's elopement put her older brother Leonardo in a delicate situation. He was beginning to rise through the ranks of Cosa Nostra but could easily become a laughing stock. If he was incapable of 'mastering' his sister in the home, how could he be a leader of men? His reputation was at stake. After a month in Pisa and Bologna, Giusy and Angelo decided to return to Sicily. They went to live with Angelo's parents, who found it difficult to accept Giusy and her mafia origins and wanted nothing to do with the Vitale clan.

For three months the Vitale brothers seemed to ignore Giusy. Then one day, when she was sitting outside Angelo's parents' house, she saw a lorry being driven at full speed in her direction. She had just enough time to get out of the way, her chair was smashed, and yet she managed to see who was driving—her brother Vito.

Giusy knew then that she had to marry Angelo as soon as possible in order to 'regularize' her situation. Three months later her brothers forgave her and, in an extraordinary turn of events, all three were present at her wedding on 27 April 1991. Giusy was nineteen years old. She was soon pregnant with her first child Francesco, born in the summer of 1992. A year later, in August 1993, her daughter Rita was born.

It was at this time, in the early 1990s, that the Vitale clan grew in importance. Giusy heard of her brothers' exploits on the radio and television and through conversations: a father killed here, a shop burnt down there. In the Sicilian Mafia, violence is key to career progression, and thanks to their brutality the Vitale brothers quickly pulled themselves up to the top of Cosa Nostra, becoming henchmen of Toto Riina. With the Butcher they were involved in the organization's bloodiest attacks and murders. Among his best friends Vito counted Giovanni Brusca, one of the Mafia's most savage killers, nicknamed *lo scannacristiani* ('the cutthroat of Christians'), with more than 150 murders to his name. Among his victims was Giuseppe di Matteo, fifteen years old and the son of a mafia informant, whom he kidnapped, imprisoned for two years and strangled with his bare hands before dissolving his body in sulphuric acid. Brusca was also behind the bomb attack at Capaci that killed Judge Falcone on 23 May 1992.

That same year, Leonardo Vitale became boss of the Partinico region. He was arrested three years later, in 1995, charged with 'unlawful mafia association' under Article 416-bis of the Italian penal code, and incarcerated in Ucciardone prison in Palermo. Vito, meanwhile, was on the run, having escaped into the surrounding mountains after a tip-off from a mafioso friend that he was about to be arrested.

Giusy now began to serve as intermediary for the two brothers, who trusted her absolutely. She took *pizzini* (messages) from her visits to Leonardo in Ucciardone and delivered them to Vito and other clan members still at liberty. She told them everything that was happening in Partinico. She managed the *pizzo* protection racket, distributed payments to the wives of imprisoned mafiosi and ran the day-to-day business. 'It was at that time that I learned what needed to be known about the clan's business affairs,' she recalled. 'The more time passed, the more I felt capable of managing everything. I wanted to prove to my brothers that I could take their place, even though I was a woman.'

She could not have put it better. 'Giusy is a tough woman, determined, very aware of her role,' says sociologist Alessandra Dino.[4] She quickly imposed herself as the head of the clan and exhibited as much cruelty as the men. She had no scruples in having her enemies shot down, as she admitted: 'When a mafioso kills, it's like a butcher slaughtering a lamb, it's a habit. Afterwards he'll go home calmly. When I gave the order to kill someone I used to have dinner with my children in a pizzeria so as to have an alibi.' Journalist Pino Maniaci recalls: 'In shops she would choose want she wanted and say at the till "I am Giusy Vitale." That was enough not to have to pay. She had the arrogance of people used to bring in command.'[5]

Giusy revealed that she accepted this role out of a desire to meet 'people who count'—politicians, mafia chiefs—but also through ambition and a sense of revolt: 'I wanted to prove that even though I was a woman I could exercise power just as well as a man ... and even better than a man.'[6] According to Alessandra Dino, 'In wanting to show that a woman can do the same things as a man, she didn't realize—or didn't want to realize—that she was identifying with the same masculine model that oppressed her. She hadn't rebelled, she had just sided with the strongest, and ended up perpetuating the power that had victimised her.'[7]

For assistant prosecutor Maurizio De Lucia, there was no difference between Giusy Vitale and a 'man of honour': 'I have interrogated scores of mafiosi in my life. Now, in terms of her language and her way of thinking, Giusy expresses herself and describes things in the same way as a long-time affiliate. In that sense she is truly a "woman of honour".'[8]

The role of Giusy as a female *capo mandamento* was full of paradoxes: on the one hand, she met and discussed matters with other mafiosi as an equal, yet on the other, she was unable to go to Mafia meetings alone as this would have met with disapproval. As a question of respect and honour, she had to be accompanied by a male relative. In the Mafia, then, there's no problem with a woman ordering a murder, but she cannot have aspersions cast on her honour. Alessandra Dino adds: 'When I spoke to Giusy I always noticed how she mixed personal feelings with business, something the men I've interviewed didn't do. Her involvement in Cosa Nostra was never separated from the love she had for her brothers.'

The reign of the 'boss in petticoats'[9] was only to last three months: on 25 July 1998 she was arrested, then charged with illegal mafia association. During the first phase of her detention she acted like a man, never complaining and giving nothing away. After four and a half years in jail she was released on 25 December 2002, but was then rearrested on 3 March 2003 for murder. Risking life imprisonment, she could be sentenced under Article 41-bis of the penal code and the 'hard' prison regime handed out to mafia chiefs and terrorists: total isolation, restrictions on visits, censorship of correspondence.

Giusy admits that, paradoxically, it was in jail that she felt free for the first time: 'In prison I could read, put on a short skirt and make-up if I wanted to. My time belonged to me, not to my brothers.' She met Alfio Garozzo, a man she had known about from a year before her arrest, when they had collaborated several times over money laundering. After his arrest he had started collaborating with the authorities, and with her cell immediately under his, he began nagging her to do the same. He insisted that it was the only option, for her and her children, and that all four of them would build a new life under witness protection. Isolated, Giusy was impressionable, and in July 2004 she went to see Pietro Grasso, Palermo's prosecutor, to begin her collaboration—but she would later retract it.

Yet everything was to change dramatically the day that she was visited by her six-year-old son Francesco. 'He asked me,

"Mummy, what does it mean, mafia association?" I didn't know what to say, and replied, "It's something bad. You'll understand when you're older." This question really made me think about my life, about my choices, which in reality had never existed, and what I wanted for my children. It was for them that I decided to sever ties with my past.' Others have suggested that it was to avoid a life sentence.

On 16 February 2005, Giusy began to cooperate with the justice system. For Maurizio De Lucia, such collaboration was highly symbolic. The Vitales are a powerful Mafia family, typically Corleonese in their absolute devotion to Toto Riina and Leoluca Bagarella, to whom they are tightly bound. From the moment a woman from that family took the plunge and decided to collaborate, the psychological effect was devastating. It proved that absolutely no Mafia family was immune to the possibility that one of their members might collaborate.'

Giusy knew the price she would pay. She was disowned by her family and the brothers she admired so much. From his cell Leonardo sent a note to the local newspaper: 'We have learnt that a former blood relation is collaborating. We disown her living or dead, and hope that it will be the latter as soon as possible ... She is a poisonous insect.' She explains: 'My brothers' reaction was painful, but I still love them. I hope that one day they'll make the same decision that I did.'[10]

Giusy still lives under the witness protection programme for *pentiti* and their children, far from Sicily and under a new identity. Yet she refuses to disown her past, or to accept the label *pentita*. She wrote: 'I don't regret anything! And anyway it would be pointless as those who are dead can't be reborn. I did what I did because it was necessary and because I believed in it. If I hadn't done it, it's them who would have killed me. Informing only makes sense for the future ... for me and my children, so we can lead a normal life.'

4

CARMELA IUCULANO

FOR THE LOVE OF HER CHILDREN

Carmela Rosalia Iuculano was born on 6 June 1973 in Palermo[1] but grew up in Cerda, a small town of 5,000 inhabitants 70 kilometres from the Sicilian capital. Her family had no connection with the Mafia; her father, Sebastiano Iuculano, was a respectable businessman, building and repairing roads and motorways. He liked to tell his daughter how he was a self-made man who started out with a single lorry. He was also a Social Democrat town councillor. Thanks to him, the Iuculano family were comfortably off.

Carmela's mother was a housewife and looked after the children's education. She was hardly affectionate towards her daughter and punished her regularly when her husband was away, but she was also worried about her health, because Carmela was very thin and suffered from anorexia. Her brother, Giuseppe, was six years older and extremely possessive of her; he accompanied her whenever she went out. Young girls in Cerda were not allowed out at night without their father or brother; Giuseppe was expected, as a good Sicilian, to safeguard his sister's reputation.

Throughout her childhood Carmela nurtured a limitless and reciprocated admiration for her father Sebastiano. She was the only one allowed to play with him when he came home from work, and he allowed nobody, not even his wife, to punish her. She evoked a typical protective *pater familias*, who would not allow her to go out with girlfriends her own age, let alone with boys.[2] She was expected to obey him and to be the 'good Sicilian daughter' personified.[3]

Yet this hero fell abruptly off his pedestal when, at the age of fourteen, Carmela found out that her father had a mistress. It all began when she found a letter in the glove compartment of his car written by a young girl whose mother Sebastiano had helped in a moment of crisis. She wrote that, thanks to him, her mother was feeling much better, that he should leave his wife and children to live with them, and that she already considered him as a father. At first Carmela refused to believe it, trying to convince herself that her father had fallen into a trap. She then decided to find out for sure. One day she skipped school and followed her father, discovering that he had an assignation with his mistress in a hotel in Cefalù, some 30 kilometres from Cerda. She then found out that they sometimes even met in his office.

Carmela felt betrayed by a man she had always considered beyond reproach; not only was he unfaithful to his wife, but he beat her if she showed any signs of jealousy. Carmela told her brother what she had seen. He admitted that he already knew and was blackmailing their father. She then confided in her mother, hoping to make her react and leave her husband, but she hid behind honour and reputation: 'It's not done, it would be shameful!'; 'I would never have the courage to admit to my father that I was leaving my husband. He wouldn't understand.'

Nauseated by her parents' behaviour, Carmela decided to rebel. She starting secretly seeing a boy, but her brother found out and immediately informed their father. Judging the boy to be socially inferior, Sebastiano offered to employ him if he would agree to end the relationship. When Carmela heard about this she was furious, and the family atmosphere deteriorated rapidly to the point of becoming unbearable. She then had an idea: to find a boy that her father and brother would respect and fear.

This providential figure appeared one Sunday in August 1989. Named Pino Rizzo, he was known in the village as belonging to an important family within Cosa Nostra. Carmela had just been accosted in the street by the organizers of a local beauty contest when Pino strode up to her and announced, 'If you accept, you're no longer my fiancée.' Momentarily speechless, as she had never seen him before, she managed to reply, 'Who are you to decide that I'm your fiancée?' He retorted: 'I've decided, full stop.' Faced with such arrogance she could only think, 'Here's the young man who will stand up to my father and brother!'

From then on the young couple saw each other regularly, Carmela wanting only to provoke her parents. She told Pino that her father cheated on and beat her mother, and Pino promised her that when they were married one day, he would respect and protect her. Her family, however, soon became aware of what was going on: her father forbade her to go out, and her brother shouted that he would never accept a mafioso into the family and that she would be disinherited if she didn't end the relationship. Carmela recalled: 'One day I went out on the pretext of seeing my grandmother. In fact, I'd escaped with my future husband, Pino. Both families suspected something and started looking for us. While my father was in his car trying to find us he was stopped on the road by one of my [now] husband's uncles, Angelo Rizzo, who threatened him with a gun: he had to stop looking for me because I now "belonged" to Pino.'[4] Another uncle, Rosolino, finally persuaded her to go home, offering to come with his wife the next day to ask on his nephew's behalf for Carmela's hand in marriage.

When Carmela returned home she found her mother in tears, and her brother wouldn't even look at her. Her father asked if Pino had touched her or whether she was still a virgin, adding, 'You are my only daughter. I'd rather you entered the convent than marry that boy.' Carmela was relieved. She had achieved her goal; by refusing to contemplate this marriage her father had proved that he loved her and would protect her. Sebastiano was once again her childhood hero.

The next day, as arranged, Pino's uncle and his wife came to the Iuculano family house to formally request Carmela's hand. She was confident, knowing her father would refuse, yet he said nothing. Dumbfounded and helpless, she sat and watched a sort of negotiation process, including an explanation of the duties of a woman who is about to join a Mafia family. Because she had run away with Pino she was now destined to marry him once she was eighteen. From that day on, she would be considered a *fidanzata in casa* (fiancée at home) and would not be allowed out unless accompanied by her fiancé or a close relative. Nor would she be permitted to go to school. Here her father finally intervened: Carmela had to finish her studies.

From one day to the next she found herself promised to a man she had chosen simply to hurt her father and force him to reconsider his controlling behaviour. Now she felt more betrayed than ever, by someone she had trusted. Driven by anger, she had set in motion a process that she thought she could control and had instead become trapped. She wanted to backtrack, but with her pride wounded she wouldn't speak to her father.

She was also wondering why he had given in so easily. In Alcamo, a town not far from Cerda, Franca Viola had been the first young Sicilian woman to fight against a forced marriage, in 1965. Her family had resisted death threats and had even had their house destroyed, but they had managed to have the young mafioso in question jailed. This episode led, sixteen years after the event, to the repeal of the legal measure allowing for crimes of abduction and violence against a minor to be annulled by a 'reparatory marriage'. It was true that in Carmela's case there had been neither violence nor sexual relations, but she thought that her father, as a political figure, should have been able to exploit this reform or at least do his utmost to oppose the Rizzo clan's arrogance.[5]

Carmela then remembered another incident that had occurred several years earlier. Her father had often clashed in the municipal council with Francesco Biondolillo, a Christian Democrat councillor, unable to tolerate the latter acting like the lord of the town: on market days he would stroll between the stalls, taking what he wanted without paying or even so much as a thank-you. One day a violent argument broke out between the two men and Biondolillo had ended up stubbing his lit cigarette on Sebastiano's face. According to witnesses, Sebastiano did not react, and this episode of apparent weakness had helped to undermine the myth of the heroic father in Carmela's eyes.

Several days after her *fuitina* with Pino, Carmela returned to the vocational college at Termini Imerese, 20 kilometres from Cerda. She was in her first year of accountancy and took the bus each day at 7.15am to get there. From now on, as the fiancée of a mafioso, she had to respect certain rules: she could only sit next to Pino's female cousin who went to the same college. If this girl was not there, no boy or girl was allowed to sit next to her. As in the town, everybody at college knew that she 'belonged' to the Rizzo family. Boys would rather stand on the bus than make enemies of the Mafia.

One day Pino took Carmela to Vallelunga, 24 kilometres from Cerda, where his parents were under house arrest. On the way he explained that she should speak to them with great deference and use the formal *lei* form of address. When Carmela said that she was not used to behaving like that, he retorted quite harshly that she would have to force herself to learn and above all to obey.

Since her engagement, Carmela's brother Giuseppe had not spoken a word to her. One day, in order to cause trouble, he told his father that he had been told by the director of Carmela's college that his sister was skipping classes. Carmela swore to him that this was untrue, but, furious, Sebastiano blamed Pino, accusing him of breaking his promise to let Carmela go to school, and announced that he was breaking off the engagement. He locked her in her room, only allowing her out to eat or go to the toilet. The Rizzo family reacted by tarnishing Carmela's reputation, stating that they were ending the engagement because Pino had discovered that she was not a virgin. Carmela shut herself away in silence and refused to eat, even contemplating suicide. Pino, learning of her predicament, softened and managed to get a letter to Carmela in which he proposed a second *fuitina* that would confront the two families with a fait accompli. With the help of certain members of his family, he reached her via the terrace leading to her bedroom and the couple escaped to hide in the village of Trabia, where they were taken in by Mafia friends of the Rizzo clan.

On the evening of 21 December 1989, these friends pushed Carmela, aged sixteen, into a bedroom with her fiancé, where she lost her virginity. On 24 December, after a three-day 'honeymoon' of rape, Carmela and Pino returned to Cerda to Pino's grandmother's house, where they remained for three weeks. Carmela was disoriented and remorseful; a series of ill thought through decisions was taking her life in a direction she would never have wished for.

An official return to see her family was fixed for New Year's Day, but the reception was chilly; her brother did not speak to her and her father, apparently too absorbed in watching television, did not deign to look at her, while her mother timidly offered a cup of coffee. They left less than half an hour after arriving, Carmela devastated and Pino insulted—this was no way to welcome a man of his standing.

In January 1990, the young couple moved into a house, where Carmela's father offered to pay the rent. At once there were misunderstandings, arguments and blows: 'When Pino hit me and I cried he would tell me it was for my own good, that I had to learn to act like a good wife,' recalled Carmela.[6] Pino explained that to be a good wife was never to contradict the husband and to respect and obey the parents-in-law.

Yet Carmela soon sensed the differences between her education and that of her family-in-law, who ate like animals, were ignorant and had never studied: her father-in-law signed letters with a simple X. Even so, they were authoritarian and presumptuous, rejecting any sort of dialogue, especially with a woman. 'Their upbringing was unlike mine. If with my parents I'd said, "Father, you don't understand," he might be annoyed but nothing more, but this would be unacceptable in Pino's family. He often beat me because I wasn't allowed to say certain things in front of people. If I used my brain I was punished. I wasn't to think. It was physical but also highly psychological violence,' she explained.[7]

The transition from college student to housewife was brutally abrupt: the thought of cleaning, cooking and ironing all day depressed Carmela. When she dared to state, in front of her father-in-law, that she wanted to resume her studies, Pino hit her, seeing such obstinacy as a 'grave insult' to the head of the family. She had never imagined that she would spend entire days shut away at home and that her only entertainment would consist of visiting a cousin or aunt for coffee. 'Women didn't count in families then. They were only good for getting married, looking after the house and the children and keeping quiet. The sons received all the attention, and it's still like that in Sicily, even outside the Mafia. It's always the son who inherits the family business. The daughter might study but she has to be married before a certain age, otherwise it's thought that she has wasted her life.'[8]

Carmela was seventeen when she discovered that she was pregnant, and for the first time she saw a glimmer of hope in her drab life. Yet the pregnancy was problematic and in order to avoid complications she was ordered to bed. Her mother came to help with cooking and domestic chores, a gesture of solidarity between oppressed women.

After the birth of a daughter, Daniela, preparations for the wedding began. The day before the ceremony, Carmela went to church to confess. The priest asked her whether she had been forced into the marriage, adding that if she did not love Pino she was free not to marry him even if they now had a child. Carmela replied that it would be too dangerous to go against the Rizzo family. Moreover, even if she knew that she did not love Pino, she still hoped to succeed in changing him. The marriage was celebrated on 14 September 1991, and Carmela became, officially and indissolubly in the eyes of the Catholic Church, Pino Rizzo's wife. Important Mafia bosses, friends of the family such as Nino Giuffrè, Bernardo Provenzano's right-hand man, were present. 'Most mafiosi marry among themselves to perpetuate the family. I wasn't Mafia, and my husband's family always held it against me. They said that I wasn't made for this family and that I didn't know their rules and ways of doing things. They nicknamed me "the princess" because I wasn't part of their world.'

In late 1993 Carmela fell pregnant again, and again bed rest was advised. Her mother returned to help her. One day when she was cleaning the minibar in the sitting room she heard a metallic sound inside and discovered firearms. Several days earlier, Carmela had found a package sealed with adhesive tape in the toilet cistern. When she'd asked her husband to explain he had merely shrugged and replied, 'Don't worry, I'll soon get rid of the guns and ammunition.' This episode destroyed Carmela's hopes that her husband might be different from the rest of the family and capable of changing. 'I thought that my ex-husband could change because I felt he was more a mafioso through fate than by desire. He would often tell me: "It's my destiny. My father is like that, and my uncle." He claimed that he was compelled to be a mafioso, but little by little I could see that he enjoyed it,' she now admits.[9]

In 1994 Serena was born, Carmela and Pino's second daughter. Pino and his family, who were hoping for a son, were very disappointed, accusing Carmela of being incapable of giving them a male heir. Pino could not bear the crying of his young daughters and rarely missed an opportunity to beat his wife. Carmela regularly contemplated suicide as a way of freeing herself from an unbearable existence.

One day, Pino was arrested and imprisoned on charges of abduction. It was the first time that Carmela had walked through the doors of a prison, an ordeal that overwhelmed her. Forty days later, Pino was released and came home, more arrogant and violent than ever. For the Mafia, a stay in prison represents a sort of 'professional promotion'. Carmela's unhappiness grew by the day as she stopped eating, made herself sick and became visibly thinner. She then decided to swallow all the pills that she could find in the medicine cabinet, only to wake up in hospital after her stomach had been pumped. Her father, at her bedside, solemnly promise that her husband would never again raise a hand against her—a promise that Carmela knew to be empty since her father himself was always the first to beat his own wife.

Time passed but Carmela's situation did not improve: she was taking tranquillizers during the day and sleeping pills at night. The only thing she could still manage to do was to pretend to be happy, carefully dressing and making herself up when she went out, with a fixed smile on her face. In Sicily dirty laundry remains within the family; as far as others are concerned, one must be happy, or at least contented. It was only with her dying maternal grandfather that she let the mask slip. The last time she saw him he said tenderly: 'I'm about to go away and the only regret I have is leaving you in this hell. Life hasn't been kind to you, but you're going to have to be very strong for your daughters, who will need you as they grow up.'

Serena was eleven months old when she became seriously ill with a temperature of 40 degrees and was almost paralyzed. Carmela took the child to emergency admissions at the hospital, but the doctors were satisfied with prescribing antibiotics and sending the child home. Carmela then went to see the paediatrician and begged him to authorize an emergency admission. Serena was admitted to a general medical ward, where a battery of tests led to two days of waiting for results, during which Pino failed to appear. Carmela then asked for help from her father who, as a former municipal councillor, knew one of the hospital's department heads. He promised personally to take care of Serena, and within hours a diagnosis materialized: visceral leishmaniasis, a serious fever caused by the bite of an infected mosquito. The doctors prescribed French medication normally administered to affected animals, and the child was soon out of danger.

According to Carla Cerati, Carmela became aware through this experience that only economic, political or mafia power counts in Sicily; while she had spent days begging for help in vain, a single phone call from her father was enough to unblock the situation.

Carmela also had to endure her husband's repeated infidelities. When Serena was three she contracted mumps at her nursery school and passed on the virus to Pino, who was hospitalized in Palermo, some 70 kilometres from home. Carmela played the model wife, travelling to his bedside morning and evening with clean clothes. One day, when she arrived earlier than expected, she found a woman she did not know sitting by her husband's bed. Pino swore to Carmela that there was nothing between him and the woman—who was surprised to learn that he was married—and that he was 'using' her to help his own father avoid prison: he had been accused by the woman of violence and attempted rape after rejecting his advances. Carmela consented to accept this version of events in order to avoid yet more conflict.

Several month later, Sebastiano, Carmela's father, decided to widen his business interests by rescuing two cooperatives on the brink of bankruptcy, and asked her whether she would like to work for him. She agreed on condition that she find a babysitter for her two daughters. Pino suggested Francesca, the eighteen-year-old niece of friends. Soon Carmela's older daughter Daniela, then aged six, was telling her mother that her father often telephoned Francesca and that the babysitter would make them play a strange game in which they had to call her 'Mama'. Pino denied it all, claiming that their daughter had invented the whole thing. Just as she'd done when confronting her father's infidelity in her teens, Carmela decided to see for herself by following her husband's movements. One day, leaving work early on the pretext of feeling unwell, she found his car parked on Francesca's street; she could see him talking on his phone. When she rang his and Francesca's numbers both were occupied. When asked to explain, Pino said that he was in the neighbourhood looking for commercial premises for his uncle.

Over the following days Carmela checked her husband's phone and found many calls made to Francesca. When she demanded an explanation for a second time, Pino lost his temper, slapped her and threw a chair across the room. From then on their relationship worsened, with Pino only returning home to eat and sleep, refusing to give Carmela any money and never getting up before midday. Their interactions were reduced to shouting and physical blows.[10]

One day, very calmly, Carmela asked Pino to tell her the truth about Francesca. Her composure must have been contagious, since for the first time ever Pino confessed to her that he had married her not for love but because she was the daughter of one of the town's richest men. Now he felt trapped, he said, because she had never understood him or responded to his desires. He told her that he was in love with Francesca and that they had planned to move to the north of Italy, but that Cosa Nostra would never allow him to do this. This confession came as a relief to Carmela, who had always felt guilty for using Pino to hurt her father but who now realized that she, too, had been manipulated from the start. She decided to leave with her daughters and to go and live with her parents.

But divorce does not happen in the Mafia. It would tarnish the image of a boss that Pino enjoyed within the organization: what sort of *capo* was he if he was incapable of holding onto his wife? Sobbing, Pino begged her to return home; if she didn't, his clan would kill him. Carmela then resolved to strike a deal with him: she agreed not to leave him, but in exchange she wanted to be involved in his business affairs.

So it was that their marriage became a partnership between two associates. Pino explained the workings of the Mafia and the role that he played within it, and in exchange Carmela helped him to hide any incriminating evidence—as happened one evening when the police burst into their apartment. Before they had broken down the door, Pino took little pieces of paper from his wallet and handed them to Carmela: 'Hide them in your underwear. They won't search you.' These were the *pizzini*, written messages sent from mafiosi when in jail or on the run to those who are running the clan's business, and Pino was to deliver them to two local bosses, Nino Giuffrè in Caccamo, and Salvatore Rinella in the Trabia district. From that moment onwards, Pino developed the habit, as soon as he came home, of removing *pizzini* from his wallet and leaving them on Carmela's bedside table in case they received another visit from the police. She wondered whether she should report him, but she was his wife, and in her culture a wife does everything for her husband.

Little by little Carmela began to understand Cosa Nostra's structure. She learned that Pino's uncle Rosolino was the *capo famiglia* (family chief) in the *comune* of Sciara; and that this rank was inferior to that of *capo mandamento* (district chief). Nino Giuffrè was the district chief of the Caccamo-Trabia-Cerda zone, and Domenico Virga boss of Madonie-Cefalù-Campofelice-Polizzi-Collesano and San Mauro Castelverde. The *capo dei capi*, the leader with the final word on the running of the area, was Bernardo Provenzano. Both Pino and Rosolino openly discussed their business affairs in front of their respective wives, and though they were not allowed to speak they could still listen. Carmela committed everything she heard to memory.

In 2002, the couple moved to Contrada Canna, an isolated rural location near Cerda—the ideal venue for hosting 'family' meetings. This development marked the beginning of an intense social life, as a visit to Contrada Canna quickly became obligatory for all the Mafia chiefs in the area, and they received 'prestigious' guests such as Domenico Virga. A happy Pino reported to Carmela the flattering comments he'd received: she was a magnificent woman, intelligent, with good taste, a fitting wife for a mafioso. By now, Pino blindly trusted Carmela, considering her his ally and accomplice and going so far as to reveal to her all the names of the clan's members. The couple even enjoyed friendly relations with various *capi*. When in the summer Virga and his wife came to stay at Cefalù's Hotel Costa Verde, Carmela and Pino often joined them for dinner. Carmela was proud to belong to this exclusive circle and to have become, in the eyes of Cerda's inhabitants, 'a woman who counted.'

In April 2002, Rosolino and Nino Giuffrè were arrested and imprisoned, and the quarrels over their succession began. As the oldest son of the Rizzo family and Rosolino's protégé, it was Pino who should in principle succeed him, or at least replace him temporarily. He was ambitious, now aspiring rapidly to become *capo famiglia* and then *capo mandamento*.

At around this time municipal elections took place in Cerda, with Lillo Dionisi and Mario Cappadonia the two competing candidates. Giuseppe, Carmela's brother, had decided to stand as a municipal councillor on the Dionisi list. Though officially Pino supported Mario Cappadonia, off the record he was helping his brother-in-law Giuseppe. Together they visited households that they knew to be in financial difficulty, promising them a sum of money for each vote for Giuseppe and explaining what mark to put on the ballot paper to make their vote recognizable. Carmela was aware of this arrangement, because the two men discussed it as if it were perfectly natural—something of a paradox given the extent to which Giuseppe had opposed his sister's marriage with Pino.

It was still April when Carmela discovered that she was pregnant with twins. For the first time Pino was happy to hear this news, but at the beginning of June Carmela became unwell and was admitted to hospital in Palermo, where doctors declared that one of the unborn twins had died of heart failure, while the other was in good health. The Rizzo family's misfortunes had only just begun. A month and a half later, on 24 July at 3pm, a police squadron came to arrest Pino. Charged with extortion and illegal mafia association, he was imprisoned in Termini Imerese. When Carmela arrived to visit him, she was surprised to find him in good spirits. His uncle Rosolino had contacts inside the prison and had managed to arrange a welcome worthy of the name for his nephew: on arrival he had found clean clothes, soap, a towel and food waiting for him in his cell—and even a bottle of sparkling wine sent by another detainee, the son of Biondolillo, the arrogant mafioso who had pushed his cigarette into Carmela's father's face.

Without enquiring after his wife's health or asking about the new baby, Pino immediately began to use Carmela as a means of communicating with the outside world. He was afraid that the police would search the house at Contrada Canna and ordered

Carmela to tell one of his associates that an unspecified 'thing' should disappear. The affiliate in question replied, again via Carmela, that 'everything is in order', adding: 'Tell Pino that Bagheria has already arrived. He'll understand.'

Mafiosi always spoke in coded language so that outsiders could not understand them. They also often used their wives to carry written or spoken messages outside since these women were entitled to the greatest number of prison visits. Different techniques were used to communicate with clan members at large, such as the so-called 'bottle'. During visits the prisoner and members of his family were normally separated by a glass screen and spoke to each other by telephone. However, they were each allowed a bottle of water—words on the bottle's label could be circled or underlined to make messages. In other cases prisoner and family were not separated by glass but by a wire mesh, and in order to avoid being overheard by microphones placed in the visiting room they whispered into each other's ears, and always in Sicilian dialect. They could even sometimes use their own children, teaching them tricks from an early age such as making a noise or singing to cover the conversation, or even memorizing phrases when they were taken to the toilets, for in prisons most toilets were on the inmates' side and children were allowed to pass through the dividing partition.

When prisoners were subjected to the tough regime of Article 41-bis of the penal code, their mail was systematically checked, but they could always make themselves understood by using apparently harmless expressions in their letters that had a very precise meaning for other members of the clan. They could also exploit accomplices in prison whose mail was not checked in order to send their own letters, in the so-called 'double envelope' system.

With Pino locked up, Carmela's brother Giuseppe became very considerate towards her, supporting her in her pregnancy and helping her with paying for her husband's lawyer. Carmela was pleasantly surprised and reproached herself for misjudging him. Yet she knew that when Giuseppe went in her place to visit Pino in prison, the two brothers-in-law would discuss 'business', and she felt guilty that she had played a part, even if it was involuntary, in drawing her brother closer to the Mafia. One day when returning from a prison visit, Giuseppe talked to her about starting a business importing mozzarella from Naples into Sicily. It would, he said, be honest work that would allow Carmela to earn money to provide for her family.

In December 2002 the Rizzo family grew once again with the birth of Andrea. Carmela took her new son to prison to introduce him to his father, who seemed pleased to have a future male heir but remained above all concerned with business matters. His detention had made him more demanding: each time she came to visit, Pino ordered her to buy him designer clothes in keeping with his status as a mafia boss, and each visit made his egotism more apparent: he treated her no better than a minion, expected to keep the business running. During a visit where her two daughters were present she asked Pino to cooperate with the authorities in order to put an end to this existence, telling him that he could find non-criminal work locally and cut his ties with his *cosca*. She begged him to think of his new-born son, but Pino reacted as if insulted: he had not been born to become a *pentito* but was destined to be a clan boss. He had no intention of changing his life.

'After the birth [of Andrea],' Carmela recalled later, 'a lot changed. I had been alone in the house for a while, Pino was in prison, and that helped me to think and detach myself from certain things. At the same time I also distanced myself from Pino's family, who were always complaining about me and telling him I was a bad wife.'[11]

In July 2003 Pino introduced his wife to Costantino D'Avanzo, who had pretended to be involved in drug dealing simply to help a friend. Once out of prison, he contacted Carmela to ask for her brother's number. She found this strange but was reassured by Giuseppe: 'It's about the work I mentioned to you: importing mozzarella from Naples to Sicily.'

Costantino began telephoning Carmela regularly, saying that he wanted to see her and make her life easier. In September she agreed to meet him and they had dinner together. Costantino acted like a true gentleman, opening the car door for her, pulling out her chair in the restaurant for her to sit down. At the age of thirty, all Carmela had known from the only man in her life had been beatings and humiliations: she wanted to feel desired and loved. A month after this first meeting she gave into temptation and willingly accepted Costantino's invitation back to his apartment, where they made love. From then on he would call her morning and evening to wish her good night. Sweet and romantic, he called her his princess in his messages, and for the first time she felt wanted. Yet one day she found out that he was a *camorrista*, a member of the Neapolitan mafia. She was stunned, having vaguely imagined that he might be an undercover police officer, but never a mafioso.

Carmela immediately decided to end the relationship. She also suddenly felt the need to reconnect with religion, despite not having attended church since her youth. Wanting to 'purify' herself, she planned to take part in a pilgrimage near Naples, but, like any Sicilian woman, she required her husband's permission before leaving. At first Pino replied coldly that only prostitutes went to church; after much persuasion he agreed that she could go, but only if one of their daughters accompanied her. Carmela duly took the boat to Naples with her daughter Serena in a group of forty pilgrims. Faced with these people who lived honest lives, she suddenly felt contemptible, realizing for the first time that the Mafia was little more than a leech on society. Throughout the pilgrimage she was in the grip of a sort of exaltation, weeping the whole time. On the last day she got to her feet and prayed aloud for her husband to repent.

Now Carmela wanted to live in peace with herself: she went to confession and regularly went to mass, and joined a prayer group. She decided that she would stop visiting Pino in prison as she could no longer bear the idea that she and her children were used to transmit his orders. She would not, however, have long to keep to these good resolutions. On 4 May 2004 she was arrested at home in the middle of the night and taken to the Pagliarelli prison in Palermo, accused of taking part in her husband's illegal activities. Shocked, Carmela could hardly understand what was happening to her: 'I was an intermediary between Pino and the outside world. Each week before going to the visiting room I was given *pizzini* to pass on to Pino, or vice versa. But I didn't feel I was breaking the law. I was helping my husband because that was my duty as a wife. In my culture a good wife must help her husband in everything. That's why, when they came to arrest me, I was flabbergasted, because for me I'd done nothing illegal.'[12]

She was stripped and subjected to an intimate body search before being taken to her cell. The following day police officers made her wait in a room containing books, where she was allowed to borrow a bible. When she returned to her cell she found it turned upside down, the mattress on the floor, sheets rolled into a ball and thrown into a corner. It was a further affront to her dignity.

In the afternoon she received a courtesy call from other women detainees, and one of them introduced herself: 'I am Giusy Vitale, from the Partinico family. I know the Rizzo family well.' As a welcoming gift Giusy gave Carmela useful supplies: bottles of water, breakfast pastries and cigarettes. Carmela wept when talking about her children: Serena would celebrate her first communion on 23 May but she would not be there with her daughter. Giusy Vitale tried to console her, saying that she had also left children behind at home. 'You'll see, you'll soon get used to prison,' she told her. Her words revolted Carmela: she was not like the other prisoners, and she did not want to get used to it.[13]

Carmela was led in front of two magistrates: Lia Sava and Michele Prestipino. She scarcely dared look them in the eye. They told her of the possibility of collaborating with the justice system, but her lawyer, close to the Mafia, advised her to remain silent and she returned to her cell without having said a word. Even if she felt that she had acted against herself and her children, she was not yet ready to betray her husband.

Several minutes later, a female prison warder came to see her: with a child under three years of age, Carmela was entitled to serve her sentence under house arrest at Contrada Canna. She would have preferred to go to her parents', but they refused to take her in. On returning home Carmela found her elder daughter Daniela so thin that she hardly recognized her. Days passed and her daughter refused to eat or to go to school. Serena, the younger daughter, was also sad: she was to celebrate her first communion the next day but, unlike at her friends' first communions, her parents would not be present—her father in jail and her mother under house arrest.

The following evening, Daniela could take no more and poured her heart out. She told her mother how going to school had been torture since she had had to write an essay on the theme of 'legality and illegality' and a teacher had asked sarcastically, 'How can a member of a mafia family like you write about this subject?' She continued: 'I didn't say anything because I didn't want to worry you but the truth is that I'm ashamed, I'm always seen as a mafioso's daughter, and the teachers want nothing to do with me as they think it's not worth it.'

'When my daughters shared their unhappiness,' said Carmela, 'I was desperate. I asked them: "What do you expect from me?

What do you want me to do?" They replied: "Why don't you tell the truth and collaborate?" "Do you realize what that means? I would have to accuse your father of horrible things, even murder. We would have to leave and would never see your grandparents, our friends or our house again,'" explained Carmela.[14] Daniela's answer ended the argument: 'But at least we'd all be together! And have you thought of our little brother? If he becomes like our father, do you want us to be going to visit him in jail as well?'

Even if the price to be paid was heavy, Carmela let herself be persuaded by her daughters, and that evening decided to write a letter to the magistrates in Palermo, informing them that she wished to collaborate. Several days later, police arrived at her apartment with twenty empty suitcases: she had two days to prepare her departure. On the morning of 28 May 2004 police officers returned to take Carmela and her children to a secret location. Henceforth they would be part of the witness protection programme and would never return to Sicily.

The interrogation phase began—Carmela had six months to reveal everything she knew. When the three magistrates dealing with her, Lia Sava, Michele Prestipino and Sergio Lari, asked why she had chosen to cooperate, she replied: 'I did it for the love of my children. Until now I've been a thoughtless mother but from this point forward I want to guarantee them a better future, I want to take them away from that culture of silence, selfishness and hatred.'

Her disclosures were to prove decisive in understanding the inner workings of Cosa Nostra and the communication system employed by mafiosi from within prison. On 12 December 2006, the town council in Cerda was dissolved on grounds of Mafia infiltration. On evidence provided by Carmela, Michele Prestipino, today prosecutor in Rome, gathered images from a camera hidden in the visiting room in Pagliarelli prison showing how Mafia bosses communicated with those outside. Yet Carmela hesitated to recall episodes in which her husband had clearly spoken to her about his business affairs, for in Cosa Nostra a man who confides in his wife is weak and Carmela did not want to subject him to ridicule. Her new lawyer (the first had been dropped because of Mafia links) nonetheless urged her to reveal everything and to omit nothing.

A few days before the end of the six-month period, Carmela was asked to listen to a conversation recorded in prison between her brother and her husband, and to identify the individual they were discussing. She discovered that they and Costantino, the *camorrista* with whom she had had a relationship, had planned to use her as the straw man of a drug-running business: sachets of drugs were to be concealed in crates of cheese, under the cover of the legal business importing mozzarella. This revelation was devastating but it also allowed Carmela to feel less guilty about her brother, who had pretended to help her the better to manipulate her.

The trials and tribulations of life under protection now began for Carmela and her children. They had to conceal their true identities, reveal nothing of their origins and move each time a place where they lived became too familiar. In her declarations to the tribunal she said: 'I have found myself raising three children alone because my parents wouldn't support me and my husband wouldn't follow me in taking the same step. My children must be able to distinguish between good and evil. I learned to do this only at the age of thirty-one, and it is not fair that my children should grow up as I did. It is my children who give me the strength to carry on because they are more mature than others of their age. Each time that I become discouraged they say: "Mama, what are you doing? Get up, and don't worry." I miss my land, the sea and the sun, but I love this new Carmela: I feel free, normal and no longer caught in the web that the Mafia spins and you can't escape from.'

'The hardest rule to follow,' Carmela admitted to Anne Véron, 'is not to be able to tell your story to anybody. It's very difficult as you see people, even those once close to you, distancing themselves because they feel there's something strange about you. And you can't do anything about it, because you can't tell them the truth. The reaction would be double-edged: there are those who would understand and others who would be afraid.

> I would like to be able to see my home again, but I don't miss the people there, as today I feel very different from them. For instance when my mother calls Serena (who is now twenty) she might tell her that one of her old classmates is expecting a baby and ask: 'What about you? Still nothing?' That's the mentality back there, and we're light years away from it now. If my daughter was to have a child today, it would seem absurd, but if I'd stayed there I wouldn't have found it odd.

Although initially she collaborated entirely for the sake of her children, Carmela began to believe that her initiative might have a wider role in making things change in Sicily: 'The Mafia phenomenon will last for as long as shopkeepers, businessmen and politicians continue to keep their heads down and are afraid to speak out.' She hoped to become an example for other wives, sisters or daughters of mafiosi.

During the hearings she aimed remarks at her husband in an attempt to make him repent: 'I believe in miracles and I believe you have to show courage, because courage is not killing people. It is following me and choosing your real family: your wife and your children.' Pino Rizzo has shown no signs of remorse: he is still serving his prison sentence today. Carmela, on the other hand, is now a new woman.

PART TWO

WOMEN IN THE 'NDRANGHETA

Etymologically derived from the Greek *andragathos*, 'man of valour', the 'Ndrangheta has its roots in Calabria, the southernmost and poorest region of mainland Italy.

According to some historians, this criminal organization was originally composed of 'soldiers' from its Sicilian and Neapolitan counterparts, who recruited locals among the rural poor, forming a distinctively Calabrian network of affiliates. Its origins can be traced back to the 1860s and '70s around the time of Italian unification (1861), when, as in Sicily, the Bourbons used Calabrian 'brigands' to protect their agricultural estates, the *latifondi*. Marcelle Padovani explains: 'It was out of the ashes of brigandage that the *'ndrina*, the 'Ndrangheta's basic unit or cell, was born. These grew progressively more important, pushing the *capomafia*, the mafia chief, into playing the role of a justice of the peace who would intervene to defend the honour of women (with reparatory marriages, if necessary) and resolve conflicts over property and between neighbours. The idea was thus planted among the poorer classes that the 'Ndrangheta was born to protect the weak against injustices. They saw not so much a criminal phenomenon as a structure that allowed upward social mobility and the accumulation of wealth, standing in for the absent state in Calabria. The 'Ndrangheta, like the other mafias, was above all founded on a strong popular consensus.'[1]

With its rural roots, the 'Ndrangheta specialized between the 1970s and 1990s in kidnappings and ransom demands. The victims were held in caves in the Aspromonte, the Calabrian mountain massif. The most famous case was that of John Paul Getty III, grandson of the American billionaire, who was kidnapped at the age of sixteen in July 1973 while living in Rome, where his father was running the Italian subsidiary of the family oil business. Faced with the family's refusal to pay a ransom of US$17 million, the kidnappers cut off one of John Paul's ears and sent it to an Italian newspaper, with a note: 'Here's is Paul's ear. If you don't pay within ten days the other ear will be coming to you.' The ransom sum was lowered to US$3 million, Getty Sr. haggled down a little further, and on 15 December his son was finally released, after five months in captivity.[2]

Yet these kidnappings—over a hundred in ten years—drew too much attention to the organization and proved to be relatively unprofitable.[3] The 'Ndrangheta decided to change strategy, and at the beginning of the 1990s began to reinvest resources in cocaine smuggling, in alliance with Mexican and Colombian cartels. Today the Calabrian organization controls some 80 per cent of cocaine imports into Europe and its turnover is estimated at €44 billion, making it one of the country's most prosperous companies.[4] 'To do this it gradually took control of the port of Gioia Tauro in Calabria, one of the most important Mediterranean container ports, which has become a centre for cocaine imports. It is impossible for the Guardia di Finanza and the customs authorities to search each of the 3 million container ships that pass through the port every year. Since 2011, 3 tons of cocaine have been seized there, significant amounts that suggest even larger quantities have slipped through the net. The 'Ndrangheta has diversified its import channels, notably in northern Europe, where the seas are less closely monitored than in the Mediterranean,' explains Tristan Dessert, a reporter for France 24.[5]

Long considered the poor relation of its Sicilian and Neapolitan equivalents, the 'Ndrangheta has succeeded in playing on its image as a poor and archaic mafia to prosper in the shadows. Today it represents the most important criminal organization in Europe and one of the most powerful in the world: in 2008, the US government classified it among the five most formidable organized crime structures on an international scale.

It was on Assumption Day, 15 August 2007, in the German city of Duisburg, that the 'Ndrangheta's foreign presence suddenly became apparent, when six Italian nationals from Calabria were executed in an ambush just before 2.30am in the car park of the Da Bruno pizzeria. The victims, aged between sixteen and thirty-nine, were found riddled with bullets inside their vehicle. They were the latest casualties of the *faida di San Luca*, an inter-clan war that started in 1991 in the village of that name, considered the 'Ndrangheta's historic birthplace. For the first time, an internal 'Ndrangheta conflict had been exported beyond national borders to a shocked Europe.

'We then realized that the *'ndranghetisti* had seriously invested abroad, particularly in Germany, where they owned 300 pizzerias, and in Belgium, where they had acquired an entire neighbourhood in Brussels,' writes Marcelle Padovani. 'A conversation between two mafiosi transcribed from telephone taps in 1989 reveals much about this phenomenon. X calls Y: "The Berlin Wall has fallen ... Go on, buy it all!" "Buy all what?" asks Y. "Everything that you can buy in the East ... Apartments, hotels, restaurants," replies X.

The 'Ndrangheta thus became the number one specialist in property investment, in particular in Italy and specifically in Rome. In 2008 rumours were circulating that it owned the famous restaurants Alla Rampa by the Spanish Steps and the Café de Paris on Via Veneto. Whatever the truth, the rumours confirmed that the 'Ndrangheta had successfully transitioned from being a rural mafia specializing in money-making kidnappings to a national and international corporation that was particularly skilful on a management level.[6]

Nicknamed the Santissima, the 'Ndrangheta is today the top criminal organization in Lombardy, the region around Milan. Several factors have encouraged this development: the presence of Calabrian mafia bosses sentenced to house arrest in the area; Calabrian immigration into the Milan-Genoa-Turin industrial triangle; and the 'Ndrangheta's strategic decision to gain a sustainable foothold in the north of the country, for good reason— Milan represents a highly attractive market for the organization. A city of parties and nightlife, the Lombard capital is a hotspot of cocaine consumption, accounting for 10,000 lines each day and 15,000 at weekends.

Investigations into the city and its suburbs have revealed the involvement of Calabrian clans in the construction of high-speed train infrastructure and the upgrading of the A4 motorway. A report by the Consiglio Nazionale dell'economia e del lavoro (CNEL), published in 2010, exposed a very real contamination of the Lombard industrial sector, in which former 'clean' business owners, forced out by borrowing at extortionate rates, were replaced by affiliates of the 'Ndrangheta, moneylending being, like property speculation, the Trojan horse of mafia organizations in the conquest of northern Italy. More recently, a new opening presented itself to the godfathers in the form of Expo 2015, Milan's Universal Exposition. With €4 billion of public investment and a further €14 billion in economic spinoffs, the Santissima was quick to claim its share of the spoils.[7] The Italian Antimafia Commission estimated that at least €100 million found its way into the hands of 'Ndrangheta-related businesses.

PART TWO: WOMEN IN THE 'NDRANGHETA

According to Eurispes' 2007 figures, drug trafficking remained the 'Ndrangheta's most lucrative activity, with €27.24 billion in annual profits, followed by public works corruption (€5.7 billion), extortion and moneylending (€5 billion), arms dealing (€2.9 billion) and prostitution (€2.8 billion). The organization also benefited considerably from the misappropriation of European Union funds[8] and, as detailed in the declarations of the *pentito* Francesco Fonti, from the illicit dumping of toxic and radioactive waste. In the 1980s and 1990s boats containing such waste were intentionally sunk in the Mediterranean.

Revenue in Italy from illicit activity is estimated at 9.5 per cent of GDP according to Eurispes, and the 'Ndrangheta accounts for approximately one-third of this turnover, or 3.4 per cent of GDP. The organization is present on five continents: nineteen *'ndrine* have been reported in Australia, fourteen in Colombia, thirteen in Germany and ten in Canada.[9] Significant links exist with Africa, notably in Senegal, through which cocaine passes, but also South Africa (diamond trafficking) and the Democratic Republic of the Congo (coltan, known as the 'blood mineral', widely used in the production of electronic goods, especially mobile phones—in exchange for arms).[10]

* * *

Founded exclusively on blood ties, the 'Ndrangheta has produced very few *pentiti* or collaborators: one is less likely to betray one's husband, father or uncle. In June 2011, of 1,064 justice collaborators, 441 belonged to the Neapolitan Camorra, 293 to Sicily's Cosa Nostra and only 118 (or 11 per cent) to the Calabrian mafia.[11] Because of this limited record of collaboration with the authorities, we still know little about its internal organization. Yet even if it has a lower media profile than its Sicilian or Neapolitan counterparts, the 'Ndrangheta is the most deeply rooted in its territory: there is one affiliated mafioso for every 345 people in the Calabrian region.

Its base structure is composed of *'ndrine* (*'ndrina* in the singular), also called *cosche* (sing. *cosca*), small groups formed around a family whose chief is designated as the *capo bastone*. The *'ndrine* are not all of equal size or importance. Among the most famous are those named after families such as Pesce, Bellocco or Papalia. Links between *'ndrine* are generally reinforced by endogamic practices, marriage being a way of sealing alliances, resolving conflicts and avoiding vendettas. The 'Ndrangheta's organizational model thus replicates that of patriarchal societies in which the family remains the primary unit. It is thought to number some 6,000 members, spread among 131 *'ndrine* on Calabrian territory.[12]

The grouping of several *'ndrine* from a single zone is known as the *locale*, composed of at least forty-nine *'ndranghetisti* directed by a *capo locale* with power of life and death, an accountant and a *crimine* who manages the illicit business interests. Pino Scriva, one of the few Calabrian *pentiti*, described to magistrates the very complex and precise system of grades inside a *locale*. Grades 1–3 form the *società minore*, the 'minor society':

1) the *picciotto d'onore*, 'boy of honour', the lowest grade in the hierarchy given to the 'Ndrangheta's henchmen, who are charged with following orders;
2) the *camorrista*, an affiliate who has passed a period of probation as a *picciotto d'onore*;
3) the *sgarrista* or 'soldier', the affiliate in charge of collecting and cashing bribes.

Grades 4–15 refer to the *società maggiore*:

4) the *santista*, a grade that appeared with the mid-1970s creation of the *Santa*, a structure within the 'Ndrangheta aimed at penetrating masonic circles and business milieus. Composed of *'ndranghetisti* and corrupt freemasons, it allowed criminals, professionals and political leaders to sit at the same table;

5) the *vangelista*, 'the evangelist', a very high grade in the hierarchy obtained through 'criminal merit' and requiring the affiliate to swear an oath on the Bible;

6) the *quartino*;

7) the *trequartino*;

8) the *quintino* (the fifth) or *padrino*, a very high rank recognized by a tattoo in the form of a five-pointed star;

9) the *associazione*, 'the association', a collective office;[13]

10) *Crociata*, 'crusade';

11) *Stella* ('star');

12) *Bartolo*;

13) *Mammasantissima*, 'most holy mother';

14) *Infinito*;

15) *Conte Ugolino*, Count Ugolino'.[14]

In 1991 the organization also decided to subdivide Calabria into three provinces: the *piana* or *mandamento tirrenico* (the plain or Tyrrhenian province), corresponding to the plain of Gioia Tauro; the *montagna* or *mandamento ionico* (the mountain or Ionian province), the Ionian coast of Calabria; and finally the *città* (town), corresponding to the city of Reggio di Calabria.

While it had long been thought that the Calabrian mafia had a horizontal structure, in 2010 the Italian police discovered the existence of a vertical structure called *crimine* (crime) or *provincia* (province), the equivalent of the Sicilian *cupola*.[15] A chief, known as the *capo crimine*, is elected each August for one year. The *crimine* is the policy body of the 'Ndrangheta, essentially the guardian of its rules, with the power to determine the nomination of bosses outside Calabria, to establish clans that the organization may or may not recognize formally, and to sever ties. The 'Ndrangheta thus has a complex structure, horizontal on the executive level and vertical in terms of policy, mixing very strict elements of hierarchy with very broad autonomy for the grassroots units.[16] Each *locale* is granted extensive autonomy in managing activities within its territory, but it must, in return, respect the common rules of the command structure.

Fig. 1: Structure of the 'Ndrangheta

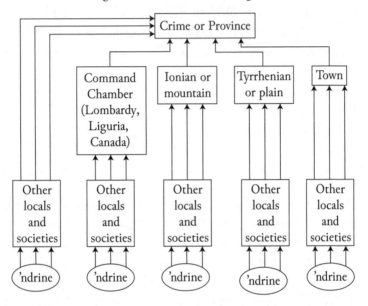

'A globalized mafia, mastering the complex circuits of money laundering and investing throughout the world, the 'Ndrangheta draws its strength from an archaic modus operandi,' remarks Tristan Dessert;[17] 'the decision-making heart of the organization remains in Calabria, in the village of San Luca, which only has 4,000 inhabitants. Perched in the mountains, this is where the 'Ndrangheta originated and it is here that the godfathers gather each year on 2 September at the sanctuary of the Madonna di Polsi.' This annual summit is where the strategies of the different Calabrian clans are decided and where the formation of a new mafia family abroad would be authorized. Traces of this meeting go back as far as 1901, as mentioned in a report by public security official Vincenzo Magione to the prefect of Reggio di Calabria.[18]

Every Easter Sunday at Sant'Onofrio and in many other Calabrian communities the sacred and the profane are inextricably mixed. The bearer's role is always reserved for the *picciotti*, the mafia's young recruits, who carry on their shoulders statues of the Virgin of the Seven Sorrows, St John and the resurrected Christ. The men of the organization always wear their finest suits as they make their appearance in church for the traditional procession. This important rite for the Catholic community represents the novices' first steps into society and an informal investiture for the bosses and their henchmen as they all process together, the young bent under the weight of the Virgin's statue.[19]

* * *

The Calabrian mafia sells its mystique through music, thanks to the thousands of CDs and cassettes available on the market stalls of little towns in the region: traditional ballads and more modern songs that tell of small-time mafiosi and 'men of honour'. The wandering singers of yesteryear have disappeared but the 'Ndrangheta still reaches out to the young through *muletta*, traditional Calabrian songs remixed disco-style. These recordings can be bought anywhere and entirely legally. They carry the SIAE label (Italy's performing rights body) and the rights of the artists are respected—in contrast with the pirated versions sold in Naples. The question has been asked: can the government combat the mafia phenomenon by sending thousands of police onto the streets at risk of their lives while at the same time banking the taxes on CDs that openly support that same phenomenon?

These songs recount the 'baptism' of the young man, his entry into the 'honourable society' that works for the good of the community, the 'men of honour' whom the *picciotti* must respect, the sanctification of the rigid mafia hierarchy, hatred of police and judges, 'enemies of the people', and condemnation of *pentiti* and collaborators; 'You ditched many good people and, thanks to you, they've arrested everyone.'[20]

The 'Ndrangheta has become an organization that specializes in constructing bunkers, secret hiding places scattered across the region. The particularity of the 'Ndrangheta is that a boss, even on the run, must stay in his fiefdom for fear of being supplanted by a rival family. The solution was these secret hiding places, from which bosses could give orders and manage their business while avoiding arrest. There are even specialists called *bunkeristi* who have developed real expertise in their construction.[21] It is often said that when a *'ndranghetista* buys a house he builds a bunker as an annex.

> Some of these hiding places are very sophisticated: detectives have found them behind partition walls, beneath farm buildings or even on roofs. They are normally well equipped (computers, television, electricity, running water), allowing mafiosi to lie low for months on end. The bunkers are emblematic of the Calabrian organization: on the one hand history, tradition and links to the landscape, and on the other high technology. That's the 'Ndrangheta: the mix of an ancient culture, tightly bound to the traditions and land where it developed, and an impressive capacity for entrepreneurism.[22]

* * *

One enters the organization either by birth or by baptism. Historian John Dickie explains: 'Soon after birth, the son of an important boss is subjected to an initiation rite to indicate his belonging to the 'Ndrangheta. The child is placed on a bed, with a knife by his right hand and a key by his left. The knife symbolizes illegality, violence, the mafia; the key represents the law, the authority of the state. It is said that if the child first touches the key he will choose the path of legality, and if he touches the knife he will opt for the 'Ndrangheta. His mother is meant at this point to move the knife closer to the infant so that he touches it first. He will then be able to join the organization officially at the age of fourteen, the minimum age for entering the ranks of the 'Ndrangheta.'[23]

Other aspirants will have to prove their worth in order to be accepted by the organization: showing their sang-froid, their skill with weapons and their capacity for carrying out orders without question. 'To join the 'Ndrangheta there is a probation period of one or two years, during which a high-ranking *'ndranghetista* evaluates whether the young man in question is brave enough: he uses him as a driver and orders him to go and set fire to a car, or kill someone. He will observe his reactions and his willingness to commit crimes,' explains Nicola Gratteri, a magistrate at the public prosecutor's office in Reggio di Calabria.

> When the 'Ndrangheta considers that the young man is ready he is termed a *contrasto onorato* and is taken to a place where all the chiefs have gathered to face him in a semi-circle for his 'baptism'. The *giovane della giornata*, 'the young man of the day', verifies that those present are not carrying weapons, as anyone attending a 'Ndrangheta meeting must come unarmed. The top chief asks the young recruit: 'What do you want?' and he replies: 'I am seeking honour.' There is then a dialogue between the two of them while a candle is lit and an image of the Archangel Michael is burned. The initiate's index finger is then pricked and a drop of blood falls onto the burning image. The chief declares: 'You will burn like this image is burning if you betray the organization. From now on only the 'Ndrangheta exists. If necessary, you must be prepared to kill your father, your mother, your brother.' The future member then swears an oath.[24]

From that moment onwards, the applicant is no longer a free man; he will henceforth have to respect the 'Ndrangheta's code of honour, knowing that he will be judged if he violates it in any way. 'For each violation of the code there is a corresponding punishment,' Gratteri continues. 'Within the 'Ndrangheta there is a sort of court where a lawyer called the "mother of charity" hears evidence for and against the individual. There is a single hearing and the sentence is executed immediately. The sentence can be death if the *'ndranghetista* has betrayed the organization, but there are also less serious punishments depending on the gravity of the offence. For example, if an *'ndranghetista* arrives a quarter of an hour late for a meeting he may be judged, and the punishment here would be to urinate on his leg, rub excrement into his face and stick his head into a toilet bowl and pull the flush,' reports Nicola Gratteri.[25]

The organization has always used written codes of conduct, the first dating back to 1888 with seventeen articles and the phrasing of an oath between 'blood brothers'.[26] These archaic rules serve to maintain discipline among the organization's members. Orthodox observation of such strictures is of crucial importance for *'ndranghetista* bosses, and crimes of honour are therefore commonplace amongst the clans. 'A man whose wife, sister or sister-in-law has been unfaithful is considered weak and can no longer be part of the 'Ndrangheta,' explains the *pentito* Pino Scriva. 'In meetings he is ordered to kill the adulterous woman and her lover if he wishes to remain inside the organization.' The 'Ndrangheta's 'code of honour' stipulates that it is not the husband who kills the unfaithful wife but her own family (generally her brother), since the shame of her betrayal falls upon her blood relatives.

As with Cosa Nostra, the only way one leaves the 'Ndrangheta is dead. Giovanni Falcone, the famous anti-mafia judge, remarked: 'Choosing to belong to the mafia is like converting to a religion. You never stop being a priest or a mafioso.'[27] And as with the other mafias, *omertà*, the law of silence, reigns in the Calabrian organization. Those who talk, the traitors, are eliminated.

* * *

PART TWO: WOMEN IN THE 'NDRANGHETA

It became apparent in the 1970s that women were taking an increasing proportion of responsibility. It was they who were feeding and looking after those kidnap victims whom their men kept chained in the caves of the Aspromonte while waiting for their families to pay the ransom demanded. According to Marcelle Padovani: 'They knew exactly what they were doing when they headed off into the mountains with bread, cheese and water. In San Luca at that time the women were the main criminal actors. After the abduction of Paul Getty Jr, the American billionaire's grandson, it was the women of San Luca who went to treat him after he had been mutilated.'[28]

Though at that time no woman had ever had to appear in court to account for her criminal role in providing the organization with logistical support, nowadays, when the police arrest a mafia clan, there are almost as many women as men. In 2009 'Operation Artemisia', led by the authorities in Reggio di Calabria, led to the arrest of thirty-four mafiosi, six of whom were women. During the investigations it quickly became apparent that some had leading roles in deciding and carrying out murders. At their head was Concetta Romeo, who organized reprisal operations against a rival gang, and Donatella Garzo, the wife of Antonio Gioffrè, an important member of the 'Ndrangheta.

The latter offers an interesting instance of the ambivalent female status, between presence within the *'ndrine* and absence at the heart of the 'Ndrangheta itself: Garzo was a respected woman whose opinions were valued, yet as a woman she was not permitted to take part in discussion meetings. Women, then, enjoy a certain degree of power, yet cannot rise up to the spheres of influence traditionally reserved for men, such as the initiation ceremony and clan meetings. At the yearly 'Ndrangheta gathering at the sanctuary of the Madonna di Polsi, for example, the jailed Antonio Gioffrè would be represented not by Donatella Garzo, but by his sons.

One significant exception may nonetheless exist in the *'ndranghetista* system, that of the *sorella d'omertà*, the 'sister of *omertà*'. This role was described by the justice collaborator Antonio Zagari in the context of the 1995 'Isola Felice' trial: 'although the 'Ndrangheta's rules do not allow female affiliation, if a woman is considered particularly worthy she can be associated with the organization via the title of "sister of *omertà*" without having to swear a loyalty oath, as is compulsory for all men.' The only recorded case is that of Maria Morello, *sorella d'omertà* for the Lombard 'Ndrangheta in the 1970s and '80s. She performed a multitude of functions for the Mazzaferro *cosca* including hiding weapons, identifying individuals to be kidnapped or helping fugitive affiliates. It is worth noting that Morello was not the relative of a member, but was selected for this role due to her conspicuous criminal past (cheque fraud, threatening behaviour towards the police, contraband smuggling and incitement to corruption) and because of her loyalty to the *omertà* code and to *'ndranghetista* principles. As she is the single documented example, however, the concept of the 'sister of *omertà*' is perhaps questionable for its lack of precise data.

In 2010, the Pesce clan, one of the most powerful in Calabria, was partly dismantled by the *carabinieri*. Six women were arrested—a sign that the time has long since past when magistrates considered women mere victims of their husbands. Perhaps they were held because the prosecutors were assuming that they would be less able than the men to bear detention and separation from their children; perhaps they were counting on the fact that women might be potential collaborators. This is indeed what happened with Giusy Pesce—unable to cope with prison, she quickly agreed to cooperate with the legal authorities. Her testimony was to prove crucial not so much for the information that she provided as for the message it sent out: that there is another life beyond the mafia.

PART TWO: WOMEN IN THE 'NDRANGHETA

Risking their lives, other women have stood up to one of the world's most powerful mafias: Lea Garofalo, Maria Concetta Cacciola and Santa Buccafusca. They were all willing to inform on their family circle in a bid to offer a better life to their children.

5

GIUSY PESCE

WIND OF REVOLT

When the police came to arrest Giuseppina Pesce during the night of 27–8 April 2010, her nine-year-old son Gaetano was pretending to be asleep: 'They told me that you'd gone to hospital for an operation, like Papa, but I'd realized that they were taking you to prison.'[1] On that occasion 'Operation All Inside'[2] ended with the arrest of forty people from the Pesce mafia clan, one of the most powerful on the plain of Gioa Tauro in Reggio di Calabria province. Among them was Giuseppina 'Giusy' Pesce, aged thirty-one, mother of three and niece of the main boss, as well as her mother, Angela Ferraro, her sister Marina and brother Francesco, together with a huge number of uncles and cousins. Her father and husband, meanwhile, had already been incarcerated for years, convicted of illegal mafia association and drug smuggling.[3]

Giusy grew up in Rosarno, a little *comune* of about 15,000 inhabitants known for its strong mafia presence[4] and thrown into the spotlight in January 2010 after an immigrant worker riot.[5] Here the 'Ndrangheta channels some 80 per cent of cocaine imports from Colombia into Europe via the port of Gioa Tauro.[6]

Converted in the 1970s and 1980s to serve as the coal and mineral terminus for a never completed steelworks, it was then reconverted from 1994 to receive container ships. In 2011 it was the first Italian and fifth Mediterranean port in terms of container traffic.[7] In 2012, 2 tons of cocaine were seized, concealed among canned vegetables, furniture or even cement blocks.[8]

'Rosarno was quite a flourishing little town until the 1980s, because it's fertile Calabrian land with many orange and mandarin trees. People made a good living. But the situation worsened due to organized crime, which was underestimated. In the 1990s the 'Ndrangheta moved from being a poor, rural mafia to become a business mafia infiltrating public works and living off the drug trade. The town's economic and social conditions then deteriorated considerably: the shopkeepers couldn't trade freely any more, they had to pay the *pizzo*,' explains Elisabetta Tripodi, the *comune*'s mayor from 2010 to 2014.[9]

Two allied clans ruled the roost in Rosarno: the Pesce and the Bellocco. The Pesce family were a veritable dynasty that had reigned over the town since 1923, the year that the clan's historic boss Giuseppe Pesce ('Don Peppino') was born. 'I have worked all my life as an agricultural labourer and the scars I have on my hands prove it,' he declared proudly during a trial in which he was accused of murder. Even if he did indeed work in the orange groves of Focoli, a little Calabrian village between Rosarno and San Ferdinando, Giuseppe Pesce also spent much time in prison in the 1960s and 1970s. When in 1991, after several years on the run, police found him peacefully asleep at his sister Costanza's house in Rosarno, he was both riddled with cancer and wanted on various charges: murders, kidnappings and illegal mafia association.

His pride stemmed from the fact that he had succeeded in dragging his family out of poverty. The Pesce clan (Don Peppino had six brothers and sisters and twenty-six grandchildren) were now entrepreneurs whose interests extended from Reggio di

Calabria to Milan. From the port to the drug trade, not forgetting extortion, they controlled all illicit business on the plain of Gioia Tauro. They even allied themselves with the mafia in Naples, the Camorra, to corrupt the bidding process for the notorious and fraud-ridden 443-kilometre Salerno-Reggio A3 motorway. Still not satisfactorily completed after fifty years and a symbol of mafia influence in the region, it has been nicknamed the 'Casal di Principe-Rosarno'[10] by investigators.[11]

The rise of the Pesce *'ndrina* has been described by the *pentiti* Pino Scriva, Salvatore Marasco and Annunziato Raso during the trials in which they were involved ('Mafia of three provinces', Tyrrhenian Sea', 'Port', and 'Achilles' Heel'). What emerges is a family capable of diversifying its activities, prepared to share Rosarno with the Bellocco clan, another high-ranking family, and to form an alliance with the Piromalli *'ndrina* for control of Gioa Tauro. Not only did they set off to conquer Milan but the Pesce family also played a considerable role in local politics—and because they liked to please and needed popular support, they very generously financed the local football team and radio station, Radio Olimpia. They showed themselves to be as open and flexible in business matters as they were murderous in 'questions of honour': a bullet in the head from a brother and a hole dug in the ground was the punishment for adulterous women in the family.

This is what Don Peppino demanded should happen to his young niece during a family meeting in 1981. Annunziata, from the Sardignoli branch of the family, had run away from home with a policeman originally from Puglia. The young woman was found and held in captivity in Scilla[12] before being taken out into the open countryside, where she was executed and buried by one of her brothers and a cousin. In the spring of 2006, Giusy's maternal uncle, Mario Ferraro, gave his mother a pistol to murder his niece Rosa, who had become 'uncontrollable'. Rosa Ferraro had always been a strong character; in Genoa, where she had lived since her teens, she had slapped a police officer and brandished a knife to defend her husband in an altercation. On her return to Rosarno, Salvatore Pesce, Giusy's father, asked her to let him use her name to open a bank account. What she did not realize was that Salvatore then used this account to write bogus cheques to his creditors. As the first complaints arrived at her door, an indignant Rosa stood outside Salvatore's supermarket screaming in fury. The response came in the form of death threats. When the Guardia di Finanza came to interrogate her about the provenance of the bouncing cheques, she told them everything. Having become an *infame*, Rosa thus had to be eliminated, and the task was allotted to her brother Marco who, horrified, warned his sister what was being planned for her. Together they went to the Guardia di Finanza in Gioia Tauro to report what had happened.[13] The young woman was immediately removed to a safe place.

Giusy soon realized what it meant to be called Pesce in Rosarno: 'I have always known, since I was a child.'[14] She was the oldest daughter of the four children of Salvatore Pesce, known as 'u Babbù' (the halfwit),[15] and Angela Ferraro. Her father had been alternating spells in prison with time on the run since Giusy's birth on 24 September 1979 in Gioia Tauro. He was not the only family member to disappear regularly and for long periods; on holidays she would often go to visit her uncle Antonio, nicknamed 'Testuni' (stubborn) and Don Peppino's designated successor, at the country house where he was in hiding.

When Don Peppino died in 1992, Giusy was thirteen, had hardly finished school and wanted to continue her studies at the high school as her teachers had advised. But there was no such secondary school in Rosarno and daughters within the Pesce clan were not allowed to study outside the village. Giusy duly ended her education. It was around this time that she met her future husband, Rocco Palaia, a young man of twenty who worked for the

Sardignoli cousins; as a sinister forewarning they met in the village cemetery on the Day of the Dead. Giusy was quickly disenchanted: 'After only three weeks together, he gave me a first slap ... the last was in front of the children, just before his arrest.' At fourteen, in search of a taste of freedom, Giusy opted for the traditional *fuitina*. At fifteen, just as Rocco was entering prison for the first time, she had her first child, Angela, born in July 1995. A boy and another girl were to follow, in 2002 and 2006 respectively.

'After the birth of our first child, my husband began to treat me and our daughter badly,' Giusy later told magistrates. 'He neither respected my role as mother nor his as father: he didn't work and didn't take care of us. It was my father-in-law who took care of paying the rent ... He used to hit me when I said what I thought ... I tried to leave him several times but my family stopped me.'[16]

While her husband was in prison and Giusy had no means of supporting her family, her father decided to open a supermarket and to employ Giusy as a cashier. After the supermarket's rapid collapse into bankruptcy she then found work in a factory owned by her father-in-law producing crystallized fruits. It was there, in 2010, that she met a man and fell in love. But Giusy was all too aware of the 'code of honour': women who betray the family pay for it with their lives. It was no coincidence that Rocco himself had told her about her cousin Annunziata's tragic end, as if to warn her of the dangers of adultery.

Giusy's uncle, Vincenzo Pesce, was quick to warn her about the (well-founded) suspicions of her family: 'He told me to watch out, that my cousins were watching me, that alarm bells were ringing.' Her cousin Francesco Pesce, known as 'Ciccio Testuni', had her followed day and night by clan members, and by now Giusy's family was aware that she had been unfaithful while her husband was serving his prison sentence. There was only one possible outcome: death. Giusy, too, knew what would now inevitably happen: 'As long as my brother is alive I am condemned to death, because he's the one who has to carry out the sentence for betrayal,' she told the magistrates.

Her arrest in the course of Operation All Inside on 28 April 2010 saved her life. Investigators accused her of passing messages (*pizzini*) from her father and brother Francesco, both in prison at the time, to other members of the *'ndrina* and of having served as a straw man in acquiring assets with illicit funds. The supermarket in which she had worked, like many other businesses in Rosarno, belonged to the Pesce family but were entrusted to fake owners to avoid criminal seizures. 'My world had collapsed,' she admitted, 'I didn't know what was happening to me. Our role as women was to help the men, to support them when they were in prison, to visit them and, if need be, to pass on information to the other mafiosi outside, to brothers, to clan bosses. Even if you know perfectly well that it's a crime, you do it.'[17]

Giusy could not cope with prison, unable to imagine her children alone and far from her in Rosarno. She made two suicide attempts, with a knotted sheet and with a razor blade. She later admitted that she did not wish to die: 'That wasn't my intention, I just wanted to hurt myself to attract attention, to get out of prison and see my children.' The nature of the 'tactic' did not escape the prison psychiatrist, who judged her state of mind to be compatible with her sentence, but he also established that she needed psychological counselling, and she was transferred to Milan's San Vittore jail, where treatment was available.

In October 2010, six months after her arrest, she asked to speak to a magistrate. As she undertook her collaboration with the justice system, she was no doubt thinking of the women in her family, Annunziata and Rosa, of her children and the new man in her life, 'the first man who ever took care of my children, respected and loved me'. She was doing it, she told the judges, so that her son could say he wanted to be a policeman without being beaten and so that her daughters could be liked for who they were, not feared for their name. 'My son had already been programmed like the others. He would also have had a future as a mafioso, that's how it happens down there. At eighteen they would have handed him a pistol. I wanted something different for him, for him to study, but [the family] didn't want that. "Why should he study? He's going to do what his father and uncle have always done."'[18]

On 14 October 2010, in a small room in San Vittore prison, Giusy Pesce started on the painful path of collaboration that would lead her to inform on her closest family. When in the course of the interrogation the magistrates asked on what grounds she could attest that the Pesce clan were mafiosi, she replied: 'It's hard to explain because they never said it like that, but I lived in that family and I breathed that air of superiority, power and privilege.'

Giusy revealed all the Pesce business interests: from football to road building, from corrupt public-sector bids to various sorts of racketeering. Alessandra Cerreti, the prosecutor who convinced her to talk, recalls: 'Giusy first of all drew us an organigramme of the clan, showing the role of each of its members. She then reconstructed all its criminal activities and revealed one by one all of the assets used to launder dirty money.' In Operation All Clean, led by the Guardia di Finanza, more than €220 million of property and goods were seized. 'We think this represented about one-tenth of their fortune,' Cerreti adds.[19]

Giusy's testimony dealt a terrible blow to the family: Francesco Pesce, her cousin and clan leader, was arrested in his bunker.[20] The Pesce network had eight other bunkers in the area—complete with kitchens, bathrooms, air conditioning and Internet access—all pinpointed thanks to Giusy. Investigators also sequestered the family's properties, including the symbol of their power, the big villa that overlooks the town of Rosarno—a profusion of kitsch and gold fittings, it was a Calabrian version of Scarface's mansion.

Giusy explained: 'The Pesce family manages and controls everything that happens in Rosarno, without exception: if a shop opens it has to suit the clan. If there's a dispute, or a murder, everything must be reported to the head of the Pesce family.' In each interview she went further, providing more precise information: 'My brother had joined forces with the Palaia family for drug trafficking and hold-ups. With Gaetano Palaia it was arms smuggling: they talked about pistols, machine guns and rifles.'

Her statement was vital, on both a judicial and a symbolic level: this was a woman who shared the same name as the family's historic boss Don Peppino but who was now prepared to inform on the clan. Her message of hope was clear: there was life beyond the mafia. This idea was confirmed by the assistant prosecutor in Rome, Michele Prestipino:

> Giusy Pesce's collaboration was important for several reasons: firstly because she was from an illustrious family within the organization, and there were serious consequences for its credibility, her betrayal being a sign of vulnerability. Then there's the fact that she's a woman, and a woman's collaboration means something more than a man's, because you have to think of the role they play in the mafia organization and at the centre of the family. This is a very significant role, one that isn't seen very often, but which is fundamental in the conservation and passing on of criminal power: women are the guardians of the rules. Even more than all the information that Giusy Pesce gave the authorities, the most serious damage that she inflicted on the organization was to show women that there is another way, that it's possible for them to escape that system and build another life for them and their children. These are often young women, between thirty and forty, who still have their lives in front of them. I think one can be sure that since Giusy Pesce's collaboration things haven't been the same for mafia families.[21]

As prosecutor Alessandra Cerreti noted, 'Giusy Pesce, a 'Ndrangheta woman, saw the state not as the traditional enemy, but as an alternative for her and her children.'[22]

A month into her collaboration, Giusy was put under house arrest in a protected location, where her children and new partner joined her.[23] But Angela, her oldest daughter, reproached her for the choice she had made: she missed her school, her friends, Calabria. She remained in telephone contact with her father's family, who, through conversations with Angela, tried to persuade Giusy to reverse her decision: 'They won't do anything to you, Mamma, they've forgiven you, Papa has forgiven you,' she kept saying to Giusy.

During the winter of 2011 Giusy gradually re-established contact with her in-laws, whose attempts at persuasion became increasingly insistent: 'They told me it was possible to come back to Calabria and forget everything, it was all up to me.' On 2 April she sent a letter to the examining magistrate at Reggio di Calabria accusing the magistrates of the Direzione Distrettuale Antimafia (DDA, Antimafia District Directorate) of having put pressure on her to become an informer. On 11 April she refused to sign her statement and retreated into silence. The regional daily *Calabria Ora* led with a headline in red: 'Forced to Repent'.

Giusy would later explain that the letter had in fact been written by her former lawyer, who was in the pay of the Pesce family. 'The letter [to the examining magistrate] was given to me by my brother-in-law Gianluca Palaia, who had received it from my ex-lawyer Giuseppe Madia. He told me to write a copy, sign it and send it. It was also sent to a newspaper so that everybody would know that I wasn't collaborating any more. It was the lawyer who passed the letter to *Calabria Ora* because he knew the editor, Mr Sansonetti. He said he was the only person who would be inclined to publish it and to support our cause.'[24]

* * *

Giusy, however, was not to be so easily intimidated, and on 24 and 25 June 2011 she wrote two letters to the DDA magistrates reaffirming her willingness to cooperate: 'I reiterate my apologies for my hesitation and am aware that I've unnecessarily wasted time.' A third letter dated 23 August 2011 left no room for doubt:

> I have expressed my willingness to commit myself to this process so that my children and I can make a better life, far from the environment in which we were born and grew up. I was, and remain, convinced that it is the right choice ... I've come to understand the importance of the motives that pushed me to cooperate: my children's future and the love of a man who loves me for who I am and not for my name. Today, even though I may have lost my credibility as a justice collaborator, this experience has strengthened me as a woman and has allowed me to rediscover trust in myself, in my partner and above all in my sixteen-year-old daughter, who wrote to me in a letter of 27 July: 'Mamma, I want to live with you, not with the others. You are my mother and without you I am nothing. I'm with you whatever choice you make.' I feel deep down that I haven't been too selfish, but if I had been braver I might already be at the seaside with my children.

On 12 July 2011 the 'All Inside' trial of the Pesce clan[25] opened at the Tribunal of Palmi in Calabria.[26] On 27 September Giuseppina Bonarrigo, Giusy's grandmother and the octogenarian family matriarch, chained herself to the railings of Rosarno's town hall to protest the innocence of her sons. The image she presented to journalists was of a woman devoted to her family, far removed from the image of her granddaughter, the *infame*. The message she wanted to send was clear: 'real' Pesce women defended their men.[27]

Giusy gave evidence from 21 May 2012. For reasons of security she testified at the Tribunal of Rebibbia in Rome, her declarations transmitted directly to Palmi by video conference. Members of the Pesce family nonetheless gained authorization to attend the Rome tribunal, and so they were able to watch Giusy speak from behind a protective screen. The atmosphere was tense, as a remark by Giuseppe Ferraro, Giusy's maternal uncle, to magistrates suggests:

'I would advise you to bring along a psychiatrist when you hear my niece speak on Monday, because Giusy needs one.'

Giusy went over the whole criminal saga of the Pesce family again: the rackets, the bidding corruption, the drugs, the weapons. She revealed that the local radio station they controlled, Radio Olimpia, was in fact used to transmit messages to prisoners and fugitives.

She gave the names of corrupt politicians: 'My cousin Ciccio Testuni told us who to vote for ... He would stand at the corner of the school [used as a polling station] and say to people, "Vote for so-and-so, he's a friend."' The Pesce family's 'friends' were apparently Pietro Fuda and Gaetano Rao. Fuda, a former senator and president of Reggio di Calabria province from 2002 to 2005, has denied all the allegations made against him: 'I have never met Giuseppina Pesce or her family and have never had contacts during my long political and professional career in the milieu she describes.' Rao was electoral supervisor for Reggio di Calabria, and mayor of Rosarno from 1983—he was dismissed in 1992 during the inquiry led by Agostino Cordova into links between the 'Ndrangheta and politicians.[28]

Giusy also referred to judges allegedly linked to the mafia, Corrado Carnevale and Salvatore Boemi. Carnevale, president of the criminal section of the Italian Court of Cassation, was charged with and convicted of criminal conspiracy with the mafia but acquitted on appeal in 2002. Nicknamed the *Ammazza-sentenze*, 'the sentence-slayer', he rebuffed Giusy's evidence: 'I have never known anybody who was part of the Pesce clan.' Boemi, formerly assistant prosecutor at the Reggio di Calabria Antimafia District Directorate, responded by accusing Giusy Pesce of defamation.

'There were internal ramifications for several institutions,' according to Alessandra Ceretti. 'Three *carabinieri* close to the Pesce clan were arrested, and two of them were jailed for thirteen and fourteen years for illegal mafia association. Through phone tapping we also intercepted attempts to corrupt a judge at the Court of Cassation. They also tried to corrupt personnel at the Ministry of the Interior by offering money. These are not people who are simply content to give orders on the ground. They're also capable of infiltrating institutions at the highest level. That says a lot about their power.'

Curiously, the first words of the accused were not used to defend themselves but to demand that the female president of the tribunal, Concettina Epifanio, be replaced by a man. 'We want Di Palmi, not her,' they shouted. For a Pesce male, a woman is not worthy of respect and violence toward women is commonplace. 'The only language he spoke was violence. I wasn't allowed to express an opinion. Once he hit me so much I ended up in hospital. I passed out and he took me to see the doctors saying that I'd fallen down the stairs, but in reality he'd hit me in the head. I couldn't leave the house except to go to the shops or see my family,' said Ilaria La Torre, Giusy's former sister-in-law, who had fled her husband Francesco Pesce in 2005.

Giusy now lives in hiding and under protection with her children. Since her arrest, a large number of Pesce family members have been put behind bars.[29] Her grandmother still lives in Rosarno, denying all the accusations her granddaughter made against the clan: 'She said things that don't correspond with reality, everything she says is false.' Rocco, her uncle, has condemned her to death: 'You have to kill a dog that doesn't look you in the eye.'[30] 'In sending mafiosi to jail, Giusy has broken all the codes, and for the 'Ndrangheta she is a dead woman walking, nobody will forget her,' declared a young Calabrian mafia woman.[31]

But Giusy is not alone. On International Women's Day, 8 March 2012, students from the Mattia Preti high school in Reggio di Calabria wrote her a collective letter:

GIUSY PESCE: WIND OF REVOLT

Dear Giusy,

I wouldn't have had your strength as a woman, nor as a daughter or sister. I wouldn't have had your strength in this city and this land where more often than not everything is silenced by fear and shame. But when someone finds the strength to speak ... the fear disappears and gives way to the desire never to stop speaking. I listened to your story, in silence. And the realization that these seemingly distant events can become so tangible opened my eyes. I, along with many other young women and young men, will not forget your courage ... Through these words we want to pass back to you the strength that your story has given us. It is the symbol of woman's emancipation. Your deliverance is also mine and that of this land.

The magistrates who passed the letter to Giusy say that, after reading it, she smiled for a very long time.[32]

6

LEA GAROFALO

THE PRICE OF TREASON

Lea Garofalo grew up in the *comune* of Petilia Policastro in Crotone province, Calabria, with her mother Santina, her paternal grandmother and her older brother and sister, Floriano and Marisa. Lea lost her father when she was only nine months old, in 1975, but not to illness or an accident: Antonio Garofalo was murdered—an assassination that unleashed the so-called 'war of Pagliarelle',[1] an internecine power struggle between rival families that resulted in a total of forty deaths.[2]

Antonio Garofalo was killed by the Mirabelli brothers and by Mario Garofalo, one of his cousins. In 1981, during a funeral, Giulio Garofalo, Lea's uncle, attempted to murder one of the Mirabellis to avenge his brother. That same year he was killed by the Mirabelli family.

At the age of nine, when most girls are still playing with dolls, Lea was forced to cover for her brother Floriano, who, warned of an imminent police search, called his sister to take their uncle a revolver that he had hidden under his pillow. In 1989, when she was fifteen, Lea witnessed the murder of Carmine Ruperto, a family friend, killed in broad daylight in the centre of Petilia. Then the counter-offensive began: Mario Mirabelli was assassinated the same year, followed by his two brothers in 1990 and 1991, one in Petilia and the other in Issogne, a small town in the Valle d'Aosta. In 1992, Floriano, Lea's brother, killed Mario Garofalo. Vengeance was complete: in a tradition from another age, still observed by the 'Ndrangheta, the blood of Antonio and Giulio Garofalo was washed clean by that of the three Mirabelli brothers and Mario Garofalo.

Lea wanted nothing to do with this way of life and from adolescence onwards thought of nothing but escape. Later she would tell her lawyer, Enza Rando: 'My father was killed when I was a baby. My grandfather and uncle were murdered. The women in the family always seemed to me to be dressed in black. We were always in mourning.'[3] In the summer of her fifteenth year she fell in love with Carlo Cosco, also a child of the Calabrian mafia. They decided to leave for Milan to build a new life and two years later, on 4 December 1991, Lea was only seventeen when she gave birth to Denise. 'We were like sisters,' Denise later declared in her depositions in court, 'we almost grew up together. We swapped clothes and had the same taste in music. Of course we also sometimes argued, as in all mother-daughter relationships.'

Lea was soon to find, however, that her companion had lied to her. The building into which they had moved, at 6 Viale Montello in Milan, was none other than the headquarters of the Cosco clan: a hiding place for the cocaine that the family trafficked. In theory, the building was intended to constitute social housing, owned by the city of Milan and aimed at helping the least well off, but it had been taken over with impunity decades ago and since been controlled by the Coscos and other 'ndranghetisti such as the Carvelli, Comberiati, Toscano and Ceraudo families. (Despite such circumstances, just months before the wide-scale Infinite Crime operation led to the arrests of 300 people in July 2010, Milan's mayor at the time, Letizia Moratti,[4] and prefect Gian Valerio Lombardi[5] were adamant that 'the Mafia does not exist in Milan').[6]

On the night of 7 May 1996, Carlo Cosco was arrested by the Milanese police during Operation *Storia Infinita*.[7] Denise, who had just turned four, was present at the scene. Lea's mind was made up: she did not want this life for her daughter or for Denise to experience the same childhood as she did: a routine of hidden weapons and police raids. She decided to leave Carlo and Milan.

Yet to rebel against the 'Ndrangheta was to rebel against her own family, since, unlike Cosa Nostra, in the Calabrian organization blood family and mafia family are one and the same thing. To leave the clan would amount to abandoning her parents, uncles and brother. Nonetheless Lea went to the San Vittore prison where Carlo was detained and announced that she was leaving him. With Carlo's father and brother both present, it was a first act of defiance on her part, but for a man, and particularly an *'ndranghetiste*, it was an intolerable decision. How could a woman think she was in charge of her own life? It was too much for Carlo, who physically attacked Lea before police guards intervened.

Lea was a strong and determined woman. In a second act of defiance, she packed her bags and left with her daughter for Bergamo to find shelter in an institution run by nuns. For six years, from September 1996 to July 2002, they stayed in this small city some 40 kilometres from Milan. Lea soon became used to her new environment, renting an apartment, finding work and even rebuilding a private life with a brief relationship. Every summer Lea and Denise returned to Petilia Policastro in Calabria so that Denise could see her father in prison. Yet both families, Cosco and Garofalo, were vehemently disapproving of her new life, while Carlo's bitterness grew with each visit: abandoned by his wife the day after his arrest, deprived from seeing his daughter regularly, he felt humiliated that Lea was making all the decisions in his stead—an unacceptable situation for a man from his milieu.

The first warnings were not long in coming. One evening, Denise saw flames from her window: Lea's car had been set alight by none other than her brother Floriano, keen to punish his sister's inappropriate behaviour towards Carlo. He considered his sister a traitor who had violated the reputations of the Garofalo and Cosco clans, and he was ready and willing to remedy this affront with yet another honour crime.

This incident pushed Lea towards collaborating with the authorities, and on 13 July 2002 she and her daughter entered the witness protection programme. She was twenty-eight and Denise ten, and then on their lives would be in the hands of the state. This date marked the start of a new life: a changed identity, successive moves to Ascoli Piceno, Fabriano, Campobasso, Udine, Florence and Bojano—a life of isolation. Nobody was to know where they lived, since by collaborating Lea had broken the law of silence imposed by the 'Ndrangheta and would have to pay with her life. 'From 2002 I didn't have any news of my sister,' Marisa Garofalo stated in her later evidence to the tribunal, 'and I realized she'd joined the protection programme. That was confirmed in 2006 when the police came to our house and took us to a police station in Pescara, where Lea and Denise were waiting for us. I sometimes spoke to my sister on the phone but she never said where she was and I preferred not to ask questions.' During their time in Fabriano, which lasted about three years, Lea had a relationship with a man and she and Denise would spend weekends with him. This episode aside, it was a period of extreme loneliness for mother and daughter.

Despite all the precautions taken, Lea feared for their security. Denise recalled: 'When her brother Floriano was killed in June 2005, my mother was so terrified that she slept with a knife under her pillow. She didn't sleep at night but rested during the

day when I went to school.'[8] Floriano's murder seemed to signal
the end of the protection programme for Lea and Denise; in
February 2006, the commission of the Ministry of the Interior
judged that they no longer faced any risk and withdrew their
false documents. But Lea appealed the decision before the
Regional Administrative Tribunal (TAR) and then the Council
of State,[9] and was reintegrated into the programme.

Yet several months later, in July 2006, Lea suddenly and spon-
taneously decided to leave the programme. This was a difficult
choice dictated by a bitter assessment: to gain the status of justice collaborator she had given everything away—the names of
the bosses, their illegal businesses, their hideouts. But nothing
had come of it; not one of the Cosco clan had been bothered by
the police. 'For unexplained reasons—problems with the inquiry,
insufficient proof—her declarations were no use,' admits
Giuseppe Gennari, the prosecuting judge at the Tribunal of
Milan, interviewed by the journalist Sylvie Véran. 'It was a defeat
for justice!'[10]

Lea's lawyer, Enza Rando, explained during her depositions
to the court: 'Lea had renounced the protection programme,
after her appeal to the TAR, because she had moments when
she was deeply discouraged. She complained that the personnel
in the "operational protection brigade"[11] sometimes treated her
like a mafiosa even though she was a justice collaborator and had
committed no crime. She was tired of continually having to
change town and felt betrayed by the state when, due to her
leaving the programme, she was told she had to vacate her
apartment within a fortnight. She was desperate and didn't
know where to go.' Mother and daughter went for a while to live
with Lea's partner near the town of Fabiano, but they separated.
After that their life was particularly frightening; without false
papers the two women were vulnerable to being traced, and at
the mercy of the Cosco family.

On 28 April 2009, Lea wrote an open letter to the Italian president, Giorgio Napolitano, which was later published in the press.[12] Presenting herself as 'a desperate young mother at the end of her physical and mental tether,' she wrote. 'Today I find myself and my daughter isolated from everything and everyone; I have lost everything, my family, my home, my work, my many friends, my hope of a future, but I knew that already in making the choice that I did.'

Resigned, she confessed that she no longer believed in justice: 'The worst is that I know what awaits me ... death! Unexpected, squalid, inexorable ... with this letter I would like to keep the hope alive of changing my sad story.' The letter ends with a stirring appeal to the head of state: 'Signor Presidente, today you can change the course of history. If you wish to you can help those who still believe that one can live an honest life in this country. I beg you, Signor Presidente, give us a sign of hope. It is all we are waiting for ... I need help. Please, somebody help me...'

The letter, which seemingly never reached President Napolitano, clearly expresses Lea's frustration at not having been adequately protected by the state, which had effectively ignored her evidence and forced her to live in hiding with her daughter for seven years—for nothing.

Suddenly Lea decided to return to Calabria, to Petilia Policastro. But first she had to reassure herself that neither she nor Denise would be running any risk. She sent her sister Marisa to speak to Carlo Cosco to make him promise that he would do nothing to harm them. But she didn't realize that she was putting her head into the lion's mouth: Carlo was waiting for a single false step on her part to satisfy his thirst for revenge. Since 1 December 2003, the day he was released from jail, Carlo had never stopped looking for the two women—and now they were coming to him.

LEA GAROFALO: THE PRICE OF TREASON

Lea and Denise celebrated Easter at Petilia, but Lea never left her sister's house, not wanting to see anybody, especially the Cosco clan. Denise, on the other hand, met her father for the first time since 2002. They discussed the young woman's studies and decided that she should finish at the secondary school where she had started, in the town of Campobasso. Carlo offered to find an apartment for Denise and her mother and to pay the rent, and by the end of April a suitable place had been found, where he provided all creature comforts—apart from the washing machine, which was broken.

On Tuesday 5 May 2009, Lea and Denise had just returned to Campobasso from Rome, where they had enjoyed the traditional 1 May concerts. Lea allowed Denise to stay home from school that day, as she was still tired. The doorbell rang and Lea went to answer. The previous day, Carlo had promised to send a repairman to fix the washing machine, and she assumed that it was him at the door. The man was about thirty-five, of slight build, with a shaven head and a large tattoo stretching down his neck from his left ear to his back. He asked Lea to show him where the machine was, but then began aimlessly pressing buttons and asking her questions that she immediately thought were strange. Stiffening with fear, she went next door to find a kitchen knife that she hid behind her back, but the man noticed it, threw himself at her and wrestled it away. As he stuck two fingers in her mouth, attempting to suffocate her, she fought back, grabbing him by the genitals. In the struggle the toolbox was knocked over with a huge crash, waking Denise, who was asleep next door. She came to her mother's aid, desperately kicking out and punching until the man fled.

Following the attack the two women were so terrified that for two nights they slept in a tent in the centre of town, feeling safer outside among people than at home. It would later be revealed in the course of the trial that Carlo Cosco had offered the sum of €25,000 to a certain Massimo Sabatino, whom he had met in prison, to abduct Lea by passing himself off as a repairman, gagging her and forcing her into his van. It was the first in a long line of failed attempts to make her disappear.

Lea and her daughter had decided to spend a few days in Calabria with Lea's sister Marisa, but on 19 November 2009 they were obliged to go to Florence, as Lea had been summoned to appear in court the following day to answer a charge of assault. A young woman had accused Denise of behaving inappropriately towards her fiancé, and Lea had lost her temper and slapped the woman in the middle of the street. As they had a little time to kill before the court proceedings, Lea and Denise decided to go shopping. Denise spotted a sweater she wanted but Lea only had the €100 her sister had lent her, as well as a gold bracelet and necklace. She decided to call Carlo and ask him to send them money. At that moment the trap was set. Carlo asked to speak to his daughter and invited her to spend a few days in Milan. He would pay for her train ticket.[13] 'My father hadn't explicitly invited my mother, but he knew that she wouldn't let me go alone,' recalled Denise. 'She was standing next to me while I was talking to my father on the phone and I asked her, "Well Mamma, what shall we do?" She said, "OK, we'll go for a few days and then go down to Calabria."'

Later that day, mother and daughter appeared before the Florence Tribunal. Lea was represented by Enza Rando, a lawyer working with Libera.[14] The two women had first met the previous year. 'Lea had contacted Libera, where I work, explaining that she was a justice collaborator. We initially met in Rome, then we had called each other and exchanged text messages,' stated Rando at the Milan hearing. That day, 20 November 2009, was the last time the lawyer would see Lea and the first time she met Denise. Trying in vain to persuade them not to go to Milan, she told Lea that Libera could help her to find work, but Lea's mind was made up: 'Milan is a big city. I'll never be alone in a room there, I'll always be among people. And then, as long as my daughter is there I feel safe. Milan isn't Calabria. I don't think anything can happen to me there.' She could not have been more wrong.

That same afternoon, Lea and Denise arrived in the Lombard capital, where Carlo was waiting to take them to the Hotel Losanna, not far from the Viale Montello address. He had pre-paid the hotel bill up to 23 November, after which mother and daughter were meant to take the night train to Calabria at 11:30pm the next day. At reception they signed in under their real names. In her evidence in court in Milan, Denise recalled the evening of 23 November: 'The three of us had dinner and then they took me back to the hotel and went out again because they had to talk about my future. I don't know what time my mother returned because I was already sleeping. The next morning I found some hashish on the table, which my mother sometimes smoked, and I asked where it came from. She said that my father had found it in the apartment of Carmine Venturino, a friend he was living with ... When I began a relationship with Carmine Venturino in 2010,[15] I asked him whether he'd supplied my mother with the hash and he answered in the affirmative.'

On the 24th Lea and Denise went for a walk in the city near the Porta Sempione Arch of Peace. Their movements were confirmed by CCTV footage. Denise stated: 'At about 6pm we were to meet my father at the Bar Marilù on Corso Sempione. He asked if I wanted to see my uncles, aunts and cousins before leaving that same evening. He agreed with my mother that he would come back and pick her up at the same place on Corso Sempione after leaving me with the family. My father and mother were to spend the evening together then come to find me after dinner to take us to the railway station.'

Police work has provided a reconstruction of that evening's events: at 6.29pm Denise sent a text to her aunt to tell her she was on her way; at 6.37 Carlo Cosco returned to Corso Sempione to pick Lea up; at 6.39 a CCTV camera filmed the last images of Lea alive. At around 8pm, Denise rang her mother, but her phone was switched off. Denise thought that was odd as Lea would usually send her a message before turning off her phone. At about 9.30pm, Giuseppe Cosco, Carlo's brother, came home only to go out again immediately. At the same moment, Carlo came to find his daughter and together they went to the meeting place agreed with Lea, but she was not there. Carlo told Denise that earlier Lea had demanded money from him, €400, and when he had offered her €200 she had lost her temper and left. After looking for her, Carlo took Denise back to her uncle and aunt. Giuseppe Cosco did not return home until 1.30am.

Denise told the Tribunal: 'I had understood everything. I knew that something very serious had happened to my mother, and that they were guilty. I went back with them to Calabria, weeping in the car while they were laughing and joking. If a person wants to do you harm or kill you, either you let yourself be killed or you pretend to be on his side. So I pretended, I didn't want to end up like my mother.'[16]

Denise then went to a police station to report the disappearance of her mother. Adjutant Christian Fabio Persurich, who interviewed her, recalled her resignation, telling the court that Denise was convinced she would never see her mother again. The searches on the ground began, excluding no hypothesis: voluntary departure, accident, abduction, homicide. Adjutant Persurich's men cast a wide net, checking all the hospitals in Milan but also those of neighbouring Schengen Agreement countries. The prosecuting judge quickly excluded the possibilities of murder associated with theft or rape as Lea was extremely wary by nature and would never have gone anywhere with a stranger. The idea that she had simply left was also ruled out: 'Lea aspired to a different life,' said Enza Rando, 'but never without her daughter, she would never have abandoned her. It was with her and for her that she dreamed of a future worthy of the name, in Australia for example.'

The investigation finally led to murder charges against six men in October 2010: Carlo Cosco and Massimo Sabatino (both already jailed in February of that year for the attempted abduction of Lea), Giuseppe Cosco, Vito Cosco, Rosario Curcio and Carmine Venturino.[17] The trial opened on 11 July 2011.[18] The courtroom was packed with members of the press, students, representatives of anti-mafia groups, but also with family and friends of the accused, who were kept in cages at the back of the room. Denise, as the key witness, had decided to testify against her father, her uncles, her cousin, her ex-fiancé and the man who had attacked her mother in Campobasso. She was sheltered behind a screen. In a strong, self-confident voice, she began:

> My name is Denise Cosco. I was born in Catanzaro on 4 December 1991. Beginning in 2002, my mother and I entered the protection programme and lived in different places: Ascoli Piceno, Fabriano, Campobasso, Udine, Florence, Bojano. We were very isolated for seven years, until 2009—seven years of fear, during which my mother took endless precautions in order not to reveal where we were living. My mother had one and only one relationship when we were living in Fabriano. It lasted two years, from 2003 to 2005, but she had no other relationships after that. In all the years we lived under the protection programme, my mother never quarrelled with anybody.

What emerged from her account was the loneliness of the two women, their constant fear of being found, and also the distress of knowing that all they had done had served no purpose other than to ruin their own lives. They were victims twice over: first of the 'Ndrangheta, and then of the state. This feeling of frustration sapped Lea's psychological health, though she 'used neither alcohol nor prescription drugs,' said Denise.

The prosecuting magistrate also questioned her about the attack at Campobasso. Denise remembered clearly that day, describing in detail the appearance of the bogus repairman, his face, his tattoo. Everything incriminated Massimo Sabatino, alone in his cage at the back of the courtroom. Visibly nervous, he swore in Calabrian dialect while staring venomously at the screen protecting Denise. She continued her narrative up to the fatal day of 24 November 2009: the failure to meet her mother, the return to her uncle's home. 'I knew that something dreadful had happened. I cried a lot but was forced to stay in that house with them.'

Denise spoke of the months that followed Lea's disappearance: 'Once I was back in Petilia, I was living with my aunt Marisa. Over the next few months I saw my father several times when he came to Calabria, until he was arrested in February 2010. We spoke several times about my mother and he told me she'd gone away and left me behind, but I said that was impossible—without insisting too much.' She also spoke of her eighteenth birthday party, on 1 December 2009, organized by her father only a week after her mother had disappeared. It was a grand occasion, with many guests, sumptuous gifts and a concert—the one drawback was that the guest of honour, Denise, refused to attend.

The defence lawyers, meanwhile, robustly argued their clients' case, trying to discredit Lea. Maira Cacucci and Fabio Massimo Guaitoli, representing Giuseppe Cosco, suggested that she was in fact in Australia. 'Denise has told us that her mother wanted to go to Australia ... what better opportunity than to leave Milan and leave her daughter with her father?'; 'I hope she'll get tired of Australia and do us the honour of appearing in this court.' Daniele Sussman Steinberg, Carlo Cosco's lawyer, continued in a similar vein: 'We have seen that Lea is a strong woman: when she has to defend herself she does so, as in the case of the attack in Campobasso. If she was really that afraid of her ex-partner she would not have expressly demanded to leave the protection programme. The only fear she had was that my client might see his daughter again.' In any case, all the defence lawyers agreed on one point: their clients could not be found guilty in the absence of a murder weapon or dead body.

The prosecution's conclusion, according to the reconstruction of events by magistrates and based on the defendants' declarations, was very different: Lea had been shot and her body dissolved in fifty litres of acid.[19]

On Friday 30 March 2012, the court was due to make its judgment. The president of the Tribunal, Anna Introini, announced that all evidence had been heard and that the verdict would be delivered that afternoon. Denise and the accused faced long hours of waiting; the press was on tenterhooks. As the court finally reconvened, the sentencing was announced: the six accused were handed life sentences, with two years' solitary confinement for Carlo and Vito Cosco and one year for the others. 'In the name of the Italian people, the First Court of Assizes of Milan finds Cosco Carlo, Cosco Giuseppe, Cosco Vito, Curcio Rosario, Sabatino Massimo, Venturino Carmine—under Articles 110, 575, 577 of the penal code—guilty of having caused the death of Lea Garofalo, with the aggravating circumstance, as specified in Article 577, Paragraph 1, Point 3 of the penal code, of premeditation. It finds the six accused under Articles 110 and 411 of the penal code guilty of having dissolved the body of Lea Garofalo in acid after her death, with the aggravating circumstance, as specified in Article 61, Point 2 of the penal code, that this was done with the aim of simulating Lea Garofalo's voluntary departure and hence assuring impunity for the authors of her murder.'

The sentencing was brief. The court recognized that it was a case of murder, but neither the 'Ndrangheta nor Article 416a of the penal code ('unlawful mafia association') was mentioned. In the eyes of the law, Lea was the victim of a crime of passion, and not of the mafia.

The turning point came in the summer of 2012, only a few months after the court's verdict. In prison, Carmine Venturino had begun writing his confessions and was demanding to speak to prosecuting magistrate Marcello Tatangelo. 'I want to confess everything I know about the murder of Lea Garofalo. I am doing this out of love for Denise. She has been courageous and she is an example for me. I must tell you how things really went.' Venturino had decided to become an informer in return for a reduced sentence. He then revealed everything he had seen and heard in Calabria and Milan, where he had settled in 2007. He described in precise detail the Campobasso incident, the abduction, murder and destruction of Lea's body—details different from the known facts but no less cruel.

It was in light of these new revelations that the appeal court opened on 9 April 2013.[20] On the same day, Carlo Cosco asked to read a letter to the court. In a dramatic turn of events, since he had always denied murdering his partner, he made the following admission: 'Signor presidente della corte, signori magistrati, I accept full responsibility for the murder of Lea Garofalo. I wanted to tell you this during the first trial but was prevented by certain circumstances.' He continued: 'I would like to say that I do not know why my daughter Denise lives under the protection of the state. Who is she protected from? I would give my life for my daughter. I deserve her hatred as I killed her mother. Woe betide anyone who touches my daughter! I pray that one day I will receive her pardon.'

According to Luigi Bonaventura, a *pentito* member of the Cosco clan present at the hearing and later interviewed by Barbara Conforti, Carlo was not merely reading a letter but sending a message to the Calabrian mafia: 'When Carlo read his letter to the judges, he started by scratching his ear, which in mafia language means "Listen", then he scratched his eye to say "Look", and finally he touched his mouth signifying "I will say nothing" ... With these actions he wanted to reassure the 'Ndrangheta that he would not collaborate and that he was personally assuming full responsibility in this affair, but in exchange he clearly demanded that nobody touch his daughter Denise.'[21]

On 11 April it was Carmine Venturino's turn to testify:

I want to tell you that today is a very difficult day for me, because I'm going to have to accuse people again, and accuse myself of having taken part in the murder of Lea Garofalo, the mother of Denise Cosco. Denise is the person who takes first place in my heart. These are not just any people I am accusing but people I lived with for three and a half years and with whom I have family ties: they are my father's cousins. I have made this choice out of love for Denise, so that she knows what really happened to her mother.[22]

He told the court how he had arrived in Milan on 9 September 2007 and lived for eight months at 6 Viale Montello before moving to Via Aristotile Fioravanti. 'One night, Carlo Cosco, whom I knew, turned up with a blanket and pillow and asked if he could spend the night at my place. He never left.' He continued:

I remember hearing of Lea for the first time when I was still in Petilia Policastro. Everybody was talking about her: it was common knowledge that she had left Carlo and that he wanted to kill her for that. Carlo told me personally that Lea wanted to take his daughter away from him and that he didn't understand why Denise wasn't trying to get back in contact with him.

In Calabria, the adolescent Venturino was in with the wrong people and took drugs. In Milan, he began 'working' for Massimo Cosco as a drug dealer, but soon he was selected for a more delicate mission: the murder of Lea Garofalo. 'Before going back to Calabria, Lea asked her sister Marisa to talk to Carlo to make sure that she and her daughter wouldn't be touched ... Her sister spoke to the boss of the Petilia Policastro *locale*.[23] In short, signor presidente, Marisa Garofalo approached the 'Ndrangheta to ask whether Lea and Denise would be allowed to return to Calabria!'

Having left the protection programme, mother and daughter travelled to Petilia Policastro for Easter. According to Venturino, 'One day, Vito Cosco told me that Carlo wanted me to buy four camouflage uniforms, four pairs of army boots and four balaclavas. He gave me a note with the measurements and told me he needed these items because they wanted to "take" Lea Garofalo. In Calabrian dialect, that means to kill. I bought everything they asked me to and I also got hold of two submachine guns with silencers. I put it all in two rucksacks before loading it into a Fiat Doblo due to leave for Calabria.'

But the murder plan then stalled. At Petilia Policastro a police vehicle was permanently stationed outside Marisa Garofalo's house, where Lea and Denise were staying. 'Carlo had gone to Calabria and when he got back to Milan he explained that he'd rented an apartment in Campobasso and he wanted us to kill Lea there.' Venturino's account of the attack in Campobasso matched the version of events presented by Denise at the first criminal trial. His depiction of Carlo after the failure of this attack was of a man obsessed by the idea of revenge, entirely fixated on a single objective: killing Lea. He described the various attempts at her murder: 'One day, Carlo told me to wait by the window and watch for Lea going out to fill jerry cans with water. Then I was meant to buzz him on his mobile to alert him, which I did. But Lea had only gone to the shop opposite and had time to return home before Carlo arrived, armed, on a motorbike ridden by Rosario Curcio.' He continued: 'Carlo's obsession did finally calm down when he realized that Lea trusted him again ... because she'd agreed to meet him in Milan with Denise.'

During her stay in Milan, however, 'we were always following Lea,' Venturino admitted. 'One day, Carlo told us that he was taking Lea out to dinner and that we should be ready to grab her when she came outside to smoke. But Lea didn't leave the restaurant.' The next day, Carlo took Lea out to another restaurant.

Carlo had told me, Rosario and Vito to be ready and available that evening. He was going to take Lea to a secluded spot near an underground passage and we were to meet him there to kill her. When they left the restaurant Carlo gave us the signal, but then he ran a red light and was stopped by the *carabinieri*. He was scared and changed his mind. Later that evening he called me back because he and Lea wanted some hash. I couldn't find any at home, so Carlo took Lea back to her hotel and I met him there. That was the first time I ever spoke to Lea Garofalo.

Venturino then got to describing what had happened on the fateful evening of 24 November 2009. According to his account, Carlo did indeed pick Lea up by the Arch of Peace on Corso Sempione shortly after 6.30pm, as confirmed by CCTV footage. He then took her to the apartment of one of his friends, Massimiliano Floreale, where he strangled her with the help of his brother Vito. The two men then ordered Venturino and Rosario Curcio to 'clean up after them'. Venturino was given the job of disposing of the body: 'When we turned on the light we saw Lea Garofalo's body lying on the floor under a couch. We picked up the couch and put it back in its place. We then turned the body over: she had signs of blows to the face and her clothes were torn around her breasts. She had a green shoelace around her neck, which she'd been strangled with ... there was a pool of blood on the floor. We took the body and put it in a packing case.'[24]

For a whole night Lea's lifeless body lay inside a van. The next day, according to Venturino's statement, he and Rosario Curcio drove to San Fruttuoso, a neighbourhood of Monza some 40 kilometres from Milan. They destroyed Lea's body there on some wasteland, not using acid as the court had concluded in the first trial, but by burning it, 'until there were just ashes left'.

In his written confessions Venturino had indicated where to look for Lea's remains: in a well on the waste ground in San

Fruttuoso. Investigators found 2,800 fragments of bone and jewellery. Denise recognized the necklace and bracelet, 'a mix of yellow and white gold', that belonged to her mother. She recalled: 'When we went to Florence we had so little money that my mother thought of selling them. We went into a jeweller's and the goldsmith confirmed that they were real gold.' Denise had also provided the authorities with a dental X-ray taken on 9 May 2007, which enabled a comparison with the recovered human remains: one of the teeth found in the well contained an implant matching the X-ray. The young *pentito* stressed that neither Massimo Sabatino nor Giuseppe Cosco had taken part in Lea's murder.

During his cross-examination by Carlo's lawyer, Daniele Sussman Steinberg, Venturino declared: 'Carlo Cosco is a *santista*.[25] The Cosco family is a *'ndranghetiste* family. Giuseppe, the most intelligent among them, manages the drug business while Vito and Massimo do the work on the ground. They have become very powerful due to the alliance with the Garofalo family.' This was the first time since the beginning of the first trial that the 'Ndrangheta was openly discussed. Venturino's testimony ended with apologies directed at Denise: 'I know that she has heard all of this and I feel bad that I may be adding to her pain, but it's thanks to her example that I am here. I am truly in love.'

On 16 April it was Carlo Cosco's turn to relate his version of events.[26] When questioned by his lawyer, he denied any connection with the Calabrian mafia as well as with the murder attempts described by Carmine Venturino. Returning to the violent Campobasso incident, he explained: 'One day, Lea and my mother argued. Lea was acting violently, with a knife in her hand, and my mother felt uneasy ... Signor presidente, she deserved a lesson ... So I asked Sabatino, whom I knew only by name, to go to Lea's apartment and to hit her, not too soft and not too hard, just enough to give her a good lesson.'

He also spoke about the night of Lea's death:

I didn't want to kill Lea, but I was caught up in a fit of rage. That morning I went to pick up Denise and her mother and went with them to Massimiliano Floreale's beauty salon. When I saw him I had an idea: to ask for the keys to his apartment, as a surprise for Denise. She had told me that she wanted to move to Milan permanently and I thought that I could give her that apartment as a Christmas present ... Later that day, when I had dropped Denise off with her uncle and aunt, I went back to find Lea [at the Arch of Peace]. She asked me for some hash and we went to Venturino's place but he didn't have any there. So I asked Venturino to get in the car with us to go and look for some. First we stopped at no. 2 Piazza Prealpi, which is where Massimiliano Floreale's apartment is. When Lea saw the apartment she became furious: she accused me of being a liar, of telling her I didn't have anywhere to live when I owned this place, but it wasn't mine because I was living with Carmine Venturino. She then called me an idiot and said I would never see Denise again. And then, Signor presidente, I saw red and punched her twice, and her head hit the couch. I grabbed her by the shoulders and this time she fell and her head hit the floor. I thought she was already dead, there was blood. I wrapped the body in two sheets ... I did everything on my own because Carmine was petrified, I had to throw water in his face to bring him round. Then I told him to call my brother Vito and Rosario Curcio so they could help clean the apartment and burn the body. I didn't want to know any more than that. That's how it happened.

According to Carlo Cosco, there was no premeditation, no revenge, no connection with the 'Ndrangheta: it was simply the killing of a woman, just as it happens every day all over the world.

The date for the appeal verdict was set for 29 May 2013.[27] Slightly before 6pm, the president of the Tribunal, Anna Conforti, entered the courtroom to face the nervous defendants and their lawyers. The verdict was clear: life sentences were upheld for Carlo Cosco, Vito Cosco, Rosario Curcio and Massimo Sabatino. Carmine Venturino had his sentence reduced to twenty-five years thanks to his collaboration with the investigating magistrates. Giuseppe Cosco was acquitted. According to the court's written judgment, 'it is now established that Lea Garofalo was killed and her body burnt and reduced to microscopic fragments ... If Carlo Cosco's version of events remains largely incoherent, Venturino's is hardly more credible ... It is impossible to determine exactly what happened inside the apartment on Piazza Prealpi nor who and how many persons were present before, during and after the arrival of Lea and Carlo.' In the same document the court also judged that determining whether or not Carl Cosco was a member of the 'Ndrangheta was 'not the purpose of the present litigation'.

Thus, once again, the court eclipsed any notion of a mafia-related crime. According to Nando dalla Chiesa, a sociologist of organized crime and a former parliamentarian, 'this trial followed a common tendency among magistrates in the north of Italy: the belief that many more elements have to be brought together to convict someone of illegal mafia association in the north than in the south. The prejudiced clichés that say "the mafia doesn't exist here" or "we don't do the same things here as in the south" are hard to break down.'[28]

Leaving the court, Denise's lawyer, Enza Rando, spoke on behalf of her client, who had been obliged to return to her secret, protected location immediately after the verdict. She addressed the representatives of civil society, particularly the many college and university students who had supported Denise with their presence during the course of the legal process: 'Denise thanks you all, she knows that you are here and that has given her much strength. Today's verdict was very important, but now we must look to the future. Denise wishes for her mother's funeral to be organized as a big celebration with many people and for it to take place in Milan, the city where her mother was killed and that brought civil proceedings before the court.'

LEA GAROFALO: THE PRICE OF TREASON

Lea Garofalo's funeral took place on 19 October 2013.[29] The woman who had the courage to defy the 'Ndrangheta now rests in Milan's Monumental Cemetery among the city's most illustrious citizens.[30] A garden opposite the building at 6 Viale Montello has been dedicated to her, while in Monza the town council has commemorated her sacrifice with a plaque to 'mother courage and a witness of truth'.

Her daughter Denise, now in her twenties, still lives under protection. 'It's the men and women of the 'Ndrangheta who should have to live in hiding, not us, the justice witnesses, because we're only doing our duty. I would like to be able to live like a girl of my age ... to study and get a degree in oriental languages. I want to love and to be happy, for my mother,' she declared.[31] The Italian television channel Rai Fiction produced a two-part mini-series on the life of Lea Garofalo in 2015. On 19 December 2014, the Court of Cassation upheld the four life sentences and Carmine Venturino's twenty-five-year sentence, making the judgment definitive.

7

THE LAND OF SUICIDES

Her mouth was burnt, her larynx and oesophagus necrotized, her stomach perforated. Maria Concetta Cacciola, known as Cetta, ended her days on 20 August 2001 by swallowing sulphuric acid. The police found her body on the tiled floor of her bathroom.[1]

According to the prosecuting magistrates[2] at the Tribunal of Palmi, it was 'the serious and repeated abuse inflicted by her family' that pushed the young woman to suicide.

Maria Concetta, a distant cousin of Giusy Pesce, was also born into a 'ndranghetista family in Rosarno. Her father, Michele Cacciola, was the brother-in-law of the boss Gregorio Bellocco.[3] He had an illustrious criminal track record, and Maria Concetta's brother Giuseppe was successfully following in his father's footsteps with various convictions for mafia association, extortionate moneylending and arms trafficking.[4] From childhood Maria Concetta had felt the weight of the rigid rules laid down by her family. Shut up in the house, accompanied wherever she went, she thought she had glimpsed the prospect of freedom when Salvatore Figliuzzi, a local boy, took an interest in her. She was thirteen, and her parents had no objections provided that everything happened 'according to the rules': after the traditional *fuitina* the wedding was celebrated.

It was not long before Maria Concetta realized that she did not love her husband and that he felt nothing for her: he had only married her to join the Cacciola clan. Salvatore was far from a considerate and attentive husband: during a banal argument he held a revolver to her head to silence her. Terrified, she took refuge with her family looking for support, but her father's reaction was not remotely what she had anticipated; he observed coldly, 'It's your marriage and you'll have to put up with it.' As a married woman, in Michele Cacciola's view, his daughter had to bend to her husband's will; her own happiness did not count.

Maria Concetta resigned herself to her existence, miserable but kept going by the thought of her three children, the first of whom was born when she was only fourteen. In 2005 her husband was sentenced to eight years in prison in the 'Wild Wood' trial.[5] Now alone, she came under the surveillance of the men in her family, a task that they undertook with enthusiasm. In the letters she sent to her jailed husband she complained of her isolation: 'I go out in the morning to take the children to school but I can't mix with anyone. What is the point of my life if I can't see anybody?' she wrote in November 2007.

Life went on in its suffocating monotony. The apartment in which the young woman lived with her children was above that of her parents and became her everyday prison. The only escape she could find was virtual: thanks to Facebook, she met a Calabrian man working in Germany, and soon 'Nemi' fell under the spell of 'Prince 484'. They never met, but from June 2010 a flurry of anonymous letters arrived at the Cacciola home denouncing Maria Concetta's clandestine relationship. The prison bars, it seemed, had not worked: their daughter had still managed to 'cover the family with shame'. Soon, everybody in Rosarno had heard the news, and the fact that it was a platonic relationship made no difference for the Cacciola household. Maria Concetta's father and brother were furious, demanding to know whether the story was true, and when she not only refused to deny it but also insisted that she wanted to leave her husband, it was too much for the two men, who beat her to the point of breaking a rib. There was no question of taking her to hospital, however; she was treated at home by a compliant doctor, an uncle of Michele Bellocco, the notorious mafioso, and stayed in bed for three months without so much as an X-ray.

From that day, Maria Concetta lived in a state of terror. She knew the laws of the clan: for betraying her husband and dishonouring her family, she would have to pay with her life. In particular, she feared her brother Giuseppe: 'At any moment he could say "come with me" and I know he would get rid of me ... He was waiting to find out the man's name so he could kill us both.'[6]

It was in this state of mind that Maria Concetta walked into the police station in Rosarno for the first time on 11 May 2011. Her older son had had his scooter stolen and she had come to report the theft. Outside, her father-in-law was waiting for her, as she was not allowed to leave the house alone. Face to face with a woman police officer, she instinctively asked for help, confessing that she felt in danger and wanted to leave Rosarno. The police were able to call her back for several meetings and point her towards the Antimafia Directorate in Reggio di Calabria, and it was there that she started her collaboration with the authorities in exchange for protection. She provided investigating magistrates with information on her family's criminal assets and on the location of two bunkers.

The magistrates recalled 'a strong and determined woman who wanted a new life for her and her children'. Yet at the end of May she left on her own for a protected location, entrusting her children to her mother: 'If I take them away by force, they will hate me, which is what happened to Giusy Pesce,' she explained. In a farewell letter to her mother, Anna Rosalbo Lazzaro, she wrote:

You are a mother and only you can understand a daughter ... I know how much pain I am causing you but if I explain everything you'll understand. I didn't want to leave without you knowing everything. So many times I've wanted to talk to you, but backed out to avoid hurting you. I turned my pain into rage and lashed out at the person I love the most, you, and that is why I am entrusting you with my children, but, I beg you, don't make the same mistake that I made, give them a better life than mine, married at thirteen just to have a little freedom ... I thought I was invincible but in reality I ruined my life, because I don't love him and he doesn't love me, and you know it. I beg you, don't make the same mistake as you did with me, give them some space.

Maria Concetta wanted a different future for her children:

Deep down, I am alone ... I didn't want luxury and money but the sense of peace and love that you feel when you make a sacrifice. Life has offered me only suffering. The most beautiful thing I've ever had is my children and I will carry them within my heart. It pains me to entrust them to you, a pain that nobody can take away ... But I must find inner peace. I only say to you that where I am going I will have that peace. Don't look for me, or they will cause you problems ... I know that I will never see you again because of this notion of "honour" that the family upholds and due to which you have lost a daughter. Mother, farewell, forgive me, forgive me if you can.

During the night of 29–30 May 2011, Maria Concetta was transferred to a protected location in Cassano all'Ionio,[7] then to Bolzano and finally to Genoa. But her new, free life was not to last: she missed her children terribly and was soon in contact with her mother to speak to them, despite the strict rules of the protection programme. On 2 August she told her mother where she was and said she wanted to meet her. It was all her parents had been waiting for, and that evening, after they had driven to Genoa, she was on her way back to Calabria. In the car, they reassured her: 'You'll see that in a couple of weeks nobody will be talking about us any more, don't worry.' Yet at Reggio Emilia, where they were to spend the night, she had second thoughts and contacted the protection services: 'I'm afraid of going back home,' she admitted on the telephone to her Calabrian partner. But this change of heart could not withstand the desperate weeping of her younger daughter, brought along by her parents to persuade her to return home. By 9 August she was back in Calabria.

Maria Concetta would soon realize that she had returned to a sort of hell: her parents sent a multitude of lawyers to convince her to retract her confession. In the office of the lawyer Vittorio Pisani, she recorded a long monologue in which she withdrew the declarations made to the magistrates: 'My name is Maria Concetta Cacciola, today is 12 August, and I wish to clarify what happened this May.' She declared that she had made everything up to take revenge for abuses inflicted by her father and brother, and that she had made false declarations simply so that she could leave her family. 'I've been back with my father and mother, my brother and my children for three days now, and I have found the serenity that I had lost.'

In reality, Maria Concetta did not believe a word of what she said, as is proven by the calls she made on 17 and 18 August to the police in Rosarno, asking to be readmitted into the protection programme. The problem was finding a way of leaving the house discreetly without her parents, who were watching her constantly, noticing. She also feared for her mother's safety, as she had been ordered by her husband to follow their daughter's slightest movement, and Maria Concetta was worried that the men of the family would direct their anger at her mother if she managed to flee. She asked the police to come and collect her at night, before deciding to postpone her departure by a couple of days as her younger daughter was ill. But at 7pm on 20 August 2011, she locked herself in the bathroom and swallowed acid.

Before they had even buried her, Maria Concetta's parents had visited the public prosecutor in Palmi to lodge a legal complaint against X containing serious allegations against magistrates at

Reggio di Calabria's Antimafia District Directorate, whom it called 'guilty' of having betrayed their daughter 'with the promise of a hypothetical protection from ordinary personal and family problems'. 'In recent days our daughter had mentioned to us her statements to the magistrates,' read the complaint. 'She had described them as exaggerated, explaining that they were intended to attract the magistrates' sympathy, and that they had sometimes been suggested to her by these same magistrates.' The document presented Maria Concetta as a fragile woman, easily manipulated—her statements were reduced by her parents to pure inventions. 'We have always supported our daughter and her children financially,' they claimed. 'They always lived in a loving and affectionate environment.'

Fulvio Accursi, investigating judge at the Tribunal of Palmi, presented a very different reality when, in February 2012, he ordered the arrest of Michele and Giuseppe Cacciola and the house arrest of Anna Rosalbo Lazzaro. He accused them of having pushed Maria Concetta to suicide by subjecting her to intolerable psychological pressure and repeated abuse in a bid to force her to retract her statements. He described her family environment as a 'system of abhorrent values in which the "honour" of the family was elevated as a principle superior to that of the dignity of the individual or respect for fundamental rights such as freedom and the right to autonomy'.

The trial of Maria Concetta's family opened on 29 November 2012. On 26 August 2014, the Court of Cassation upheld the prison sentences under appeal: four and a half years for her father, four years for her brother and two years for her mother. Vittorio Pisani, the family's lawyer who had also been jailed, decided to collaborate with authorities.

Justice was served for Maria Concetta Cacciola, but not every woman in her situation has been so lucky.

* * *

According to her close family, Santa Buccafusca, known as 'Tita' and aged thirty-eight, also suffered from 'depression'.[8] The wife of Pantaleone Mancuso, a powerful mafia boss in the Calabrian province of Vibo Valentia, she had decided to start collaborating with the authorities after the birth of her son. On 14 March 2011, she went with her son of sixteen months to the police station at Nicotera Marina, intending to reveal everything about her husband's criminal activities: she knew the 'Ndrangheta from the inside, having been present at the meetings with the clan affiliates organized by Mancuso and held in their home.[9] Quickly discovering her whereabouts, Mancuso family members rushed to the police station brandishing Tita's medical certificates: she suffered from psychological problems and could not be considered a reliable witness.[10]

In the meantime, Tita had been taken undercover to the Antimafia District Directorate in Catanzaro to be interviewed. But when the moment came to sign her statement, in the grip of a serious internal crisis, she refused to go any further. She asked the police officers for authorization to call her sister, who encouraged her not to sign. After several days of internment in the psychiatric hospital at Polistena, Tita finally returned to her husband.[11] On 16 April she ingested a bottle of sulphuric acid and died two days later in a hospital in Reggio di Calabria.

An investigation was opened against X on the grounds of incitement to suicide, but to this day the prosecuting magistrate lacks sufficient evidence to incriminate the Mancuso family.[12]

* * *

The deaths of Maria Concetta and Tita were atrocious, but not in vain: their courage, together with that of Giusy Pesce, Lea Garofalo and her daughter Denise Cosco, has allowed women from within the 'Ndrangheta to show what they are capable of. 'Women today do not simply have a formal role, but are the real guardians of power within Calabrian mafia families,' believes Michele Prestipino, former assistant prosecutor at the DDA in Reggio di Calabria.[13] Hence the fear among the *cosche*, the 'Ndrangheta's clans, of a 'pink revolution' that might threaten their stability.

For Nadia Furnari, founder of the Associazone Antimafia Rita Atria, the case of Maria Concetta reveals the shortcomings of the religious and civil authorities: 'She was married at thirteen, and it was a priest who officiated at the ceremony. Is it right that he allowed such a young girl to be married? Maria Concetta lived in Rosarno. Did the administrative authorities in the town never set up a system for monitoring and protecting minors? Did social workers, doctors and civil groups never notice the violence inflicted on Maria Concetta?'

This appeal to collective responsibility was heeded by Matteo Cosenza, editor of the *Quotidiano della Calabria*, who in 2012 dedicated an 8 March International Women's Day issue to Giuseppina Pesce, Lea Garofalo and Maria Concetta Cacciola, to offer 'a positive and militant image' of Calabria.

PART THREE

WOMEN IN THE CAMORRA

'Power, money, giving orders, social status ... all of these are stronger than love of the family. Even for women.'

Rosaria Capacchione, anti-mafia journalist

Just as Cosa Nostra is exclusively attached to Sicily, so the Camorra reigns over Naples and its surrounding area. In 2007 and 2008, its notoriety spread across the world with a bestselling book by Roberto Saviano and with a much publicized waste management crisis in the city, manipulated by the organization. Since then the region of Campania has regularly hit headlines across Europe: tons of filth piled up in streets, furious locals setting fire to rubbish heaps, a dramatic ecological and health emergency. Behind this apocalyptic scenario lurks the half-hidden presence of the Camorra.

The deadly impact of this organization goes beyond piles of rubbish. In his book *Gomorrah*, later turned into a film and television series,[1] the journalist Roberto Saviano exposed the power of the Camorra clans and the mafia system active in all sectors of the regional economy. These clans are not only involved in running illegal rackets such as prostitution and extortion, but also in corrupt public-sector contracts and procurement.[2] Nor is recruitment a challenge in a city where, according to the Italian National Institute for Statistics (ISTAT), youth unemployment is at 47 per cent. The organization is so powerful in Naples that it has become the region's leading employer. People do not refer to 'the Camorra' as such, but rather to o' Sistema, the system. 'The word "Camorra" does not exist, it is a word used by cops, magistrates, journalists and scriptwriters. The word the clan members use for it is "system": an eloquent term suggesting a mechanism rather than a structure.'[3]

The book and its adaptations enjoyed worldwide success; it was translated into fifty-two languages, and Saviano became an international anti-mafia icon. In Naples he was seen as a troublemaker, more of a novelist than an investigative journalist for some, an imposter or even a talented businessman for others, but regardless of the debate, *Gomorrah* did do one thing: it offered a clear-sighted look at this region tormented by an evil that has destroyed its land and its youth.

Discussing the Camorra is more problematic than discussing Cosa Nostra and the 'Ndrangheta, as there is not one single Camorra but a multiplicity of Camorras.[4] Unlike other mafias, its structure is horizontal, with numerous families running their territories as they please. There is no chief at the head of the organization as with Cosa Nostra, nor a body charged with regulating the behaviour of each clan as exists within the 'Ndrangheta. The Camorra has developed as successfully in Naples itself as in the region. An urban mafia, built on promiscuity, has been born in the city centre, reflecting its narrow alleys—chaotic, but also more modern than its regional rural equivalent, which is more rooted in tradition, more isolated and more closely modelled on the Sicilian and Calabrian mafias. On Campanian soil, among the most fertile in Europe (thanks to Vesuvius), the *camorrista* plays the role of mediator in local conflicts but also, and above all, that of intermediary in agricultural commerce. He is the one who fixes the price of fruit and vegetables in the absence of a regulated market—making a considerable profit in the process.

This lack of structure and cohesion has prevented the Camorra from achieving the sort of international power wielded by Cosa Nostra in the past and by the 'Ndrangheta today. Conversely, the non-existence of a rigid hierarchy has allowed it to give more room to women, who have always played an important part in the clans' business affairs. According to Giuseppe Narducci, a magistrate at Naples' anti-mafia public prosecutor's office, 'One can't talk about the Camorra without talking about its women. They've always played a major role, right from the start.' Whereas in Cosa Nostra and the 'Ndrangheta women remain in the shadows, those in the Camorra have always been much more visible, occupying recognized positions within the clans. Since the birth of the *camorrista* phenomenon in Naples they have— perhaps even more than men—had a significant role in illegal street activities such as selling contraband cigarettes, and now drugs, and they also control the clan's territory. They often give orders and manage certain aspects of business, and though it is rare for them to take part in murders, they have been known to order them.

This female role in the clans' affairs is not a new development linked to women's emancipation in wider society, but is explained by the very essence of the Camorra's organization: its lack of structure and hierarchy, and its urban character. Yet if they reach such important levels of responsibility, it is never independently and of their own volition, but as a wife, a sister, a daughter or even a mistress. When they marry a *camorrista* they are making a conscious life choice, often motivated by economic factors or because they come from the same milieu, since marriages are most often between members of mafia families. Once they enter the family they know that they must participate actively in the life of the clan, not just as passive custodians of traditions and of *omertà* but also as protagonists in their own right. Their influence and power will very often increase with the death or imprisonment of a brother or husband.[5]

* * *

The Camorra was born at the beginning of the nineteenth century after the abortive revolution of 1799 and is the oldest of the Italian mafias. At that time Naples was the third most populated city in Europe after London and Paris. The kingdom of Naples was also one of Europe's most socially and economically backward regions. Overpopulated and without natural resources, it lacked a real industrial infrastructure, producing mainly luxury items and services that required specialist skills, offering little employment to the unskilled working class. Naples did not undergo an industrial revolution, which would have driven the proletariat out of the city centre into the urban periphery; as such, unlike in London and Paris, the working class remained—and remains today—in the heart of city. The rural population, meanwhile, deserted the increasingly impoverished countryside and joined the urban ranks, which were sometimes responsible for bloody uprisings.[6]

The Neapolitan aristocracy of the early nineteenth century feared these popular masses and their revolts, and decided to entrust the keeping of law and order to men of violent reputation known as *guappi*.[7] They were identifiable by their cylindrical hat, their truncheon, their red scarf and their ostentatious jewellery and tattoos. They were both mediators and *de facto* justices of the peace.[8] In exchange for their peacekeeping duties, the city's aristocracy handed them control of the vice industry, and this new social order divided the urban territory into twelve neighbourhoods.

PART THREE: WOMEN IN THE CAMORRA

The freshly formed 'sect' was organized around and inspired by masonic rites and traditions observed by the nobility. In the event of a dispute, it might resort to a *zumpata*, or duel, while punishment could take the form of a *sfregio*, a razor cut across the face that would single out unfaithful women and those who broke the established rules with a mark that they would bear for the rest of their lives. All these practices were intended to channel and reduce violence and to stop any proliferation of killings. With violence controlled and ritualized, perhaps paradoxically given the city's reputation, there were few blood crimes in the streets of nineteenth-century Naples.

Until the arrival of the drug trade in the 1970s, rules were scrupulously observed, with three main 'principles' or commandments governing the organization. Firstly, anything is permitted in order to survive, so long as a life is not taken. Naples has always shown great tolerance towards illegal activities provided that they are undertaken purely as a means of survival. Even today it is common to hear expressions such as 'What did I do wrong? I didn't kill anyone.' Secondly, there is nothing wrong with stealing from somebody who has made money illegally. In the Camorra's early days, extortion and blackmail were only used against the sources of illicit profits such as gambling and prostitution, activities on which the *guappo* imposed his levy. Thirdly, any sort of business, even illegal, can be conducted if it harms nobody. The drug trade was originally forbidden by this code of honour.

The development of the Camorra thus occurred within an urban criminality, organized and ritualized around strict rules. Violence was not to be destructive but a means of organization.

By the end of the nineteenth century, women already had an active criminal role. As usurers they lent money at exorbitant interest rates and were described at the time as aggressive harridans who would not hesitate to loot the homes of late payers.[9] A total of 578 women were found guilty of violent crimes and threatening behaviour. The criminologist Cesare Lombardo estimates that around 3 per cent of women at the time belonged to the Camorra.[10] On 17 September 1890, for instance, Sofia Proto was twenty-three when she took over the affairs of her imprisoned *camorrista* husband Francesco Martona. In charge of collecting protection money in her neighbourhood, she confronted Pasquale Esposito, who refused to pay. After a fight broke out and she was stabbed, the police very quickly arrested the murderer, fearing an outbreak of clan revenge. The following year, Maria and Anna Abbate, two sisters from the Vicara district who ran a prostitution racket, demanded a daily sum from the local brothel owners to keep their businesses open. When one such madam, Anna de Santis, refused to comply, they sent a male clan member to slash her face—and to remind her of the rules.

Up until the 1950s the Camorra was an accepted social reality and was even considered by some as a necessary evil. Yet by the end of the Second World War things were beginning to change. Naples was the first major European city to be liberated by the Allies, but during the conflict it had endured hundreds of bombing raids that had destroyed many buildings and killed up to 25,000 civilians. The economy was devastated, while epidemics spread in the streets, the population went hungry and the black market boomed.

The Allies tried as best they could to aid the local population, unloading supplies of food and medicine in the central Forcella neighbourhood. Much of it was subsequently resold on the streets, further fuelling the black market. The government stood by and did nothing to stop this, since at least people had access to food. At the same time, all sorts of illegal trafficking emerged: the so-called *mille mestieri di Napoli*, 'Naples' thousand metiers', or the art of getting by.[11]

Behind the contraband industry was the Camorra, but also and especially the Sicilian mafia, Cosa Nostra. In 1947 Lucky Luciano, the Italo-American *capo*, was in Naples, having been released from jail in the United States by the secret service as a thanks to the Mob for its help during the Allied invasion of Sicily.[12] Luciano was assessing the city's potential as a hub for distributing contraband cigarettes: a strategic location, a compliant workforce and easy-going authorities. On that basis he formed alliances with local bosses and started an international cigarette smuggling cartel with mafia groups in Marseille.

This was the first time that the Camorra had attained a certain legitimacy in the eyes of Cosa Nostra, which had previously tended to hold the Neapolitans in contempt. Certain *camorristi* were even initiated by Sicilian mafiosi in a gesture of gratitude, notably the biggest cigarette smugglers: the Nuvoletto and Bardellino clans. In the 1950s the cigarette trade provided a living for 100,000 people in Naples, notably women.[13] In *Ieri, oggi e domani*, the famous film by Vittorio De Sica (1963), Sophia Loren plays a contraband cigarette dealer who continually becomes pregnant to avoid prison.

In contrast to Cosa Nostra and the 'Ndrangheta, the Camorra operated as a criminal force on the street, dependent on its retail network, and as such it needed a labour force. Entire families took part in the smuggling and selling process, women, children and even grandparents. The 'modern' Camorra, however, really began to prosper in the mid-1970s with the advent of the drug trade. Heroin and cocaine, which were behind Cosa Nostra's fortune, generally passed through Naples. Each family managed the drug traffic in its own district, but by now the code of honour had ceased to exist, the 'principles' previously in force were abandoned, and the old parallel order that was more or less accepted by society was gradually challenged.

At this moment a key figure in the Neapolitan mafia emerged in the form of a boss named Raffaele Cutolo, from Ottaviano (a small town in the periphery of Naples). Cutolo not only wanted to get rid of the Sicilians, who were keen to control all the drug trafficking in Naples, but also to create a structure similar to

Cosa Nostra and to turn the Camorra into a genuine mafia organization with a supreme leader—himself. Its name would be the NCO, the Nuova Camorra Organizzata. Although 'new', what Cutolo envisaged was the Camorra of tradition. He aimed to revive the organization described in old texts and to reinstate the ancient initiation rites and the rules of the nineteenth century. Don Raffaele owned a palace of 350 rooms, once the property of the Medicis, where the affiliation rituals of the new adherents to his organization took place. '*Camorristi* have always dreamt of being like the old aristocracy and of playing the part of feudal lords,' explains Gabriella Gribaudi, professor of contemporary history at the University of Naples.

Yet from 1970 onwards Cutolo was in prison, having murdered a young man who had allegedly insulted his sister Rosetta in 1963. He was hardly ever out of jail after that, but nonetheless managed to enrol some 4,000 young men into his organization and to unleash one of the bloodiest conflicts in the Camorra's history. His method was simple: to give the lost and hopeless young men of Naples' neighbourhoods a role and an identity. When they found themselves in prison he would pay for a lawyer, books and clothes, looking after them and their families. Thanks to Cutolo, these young men felt important, and he became their prophet. In their gratitude, they would do anything for him. This was what was novel about the NCO: its young members were no longer prepared to kill just for money, but for a master and his ideas.[14]

Don Raffaele loved cameras and was adept at playing with the media to broadcast his messages. In this sense, the *camorrista* was very different from the Sicilian or Calabrian mafioso—where they were unobtrusive and inclined to hide, the *camorrista* was extrovert, talkative and exuberant. Cutolo also thought of himself as a modern-day defender of the poor, as emerged in one interview:

Cutolo: Look how I'm loved. Me, I give money to people who need it.

PART THREE: WOMEN IN THE CAMORRA

Journalist: So you're some sort of Robin Hood?

Cutolo: Yes, that's it.[15]

Cutolo did not deny the existence of the Camorra but was ambiguous in defining it: 'I am a man who fights against injustices.' He attempted to reformulate crime in ideological terms, to justify it and to legitimize himself, boasting of fighting for the poor against the wealthy and claiming celebrity status: 'If people are coming to interview me in prison it must be because I'm an important man.'

Cutolo tried to impose his power on the city of Naples, demanding 30,000 lire for each box of cigarettes delivered, yet this was anathema to the Camorra families in other districts of the city, who declared war, starting the Camorra's first internecine conflict. By 1980, within just two years, Naples had witnessed 700 murders, many committed openly in the streets. Cutolo's NCO was pitted against other *Camorriste* families, gathered together under the banner of the Nuova Famiglia, who refused to submit to Don Raffaele's organization. The war lasted three years. While the imprisoned Cutolo had been unable to extend his power base beyond Ottaviano, the Nuova Famiglia, created purely to counter Cutolo's NCO and now with no raison d'être, was disbanded. The Camorra went back to being what it had always been: a horizontally structured organization, within which some fifty families divided up and fought over territory.[16] Since this failed attempt to bring together the disparate clans, they have continuously struggled amongst themselves for power. A family may control a single street, but where one clan's territory ends and another's begins is often unclear. Conflicts are commonplace, while careers are rapid, brief and extremely lucrative. A *camorrista* can be in charge of a dealing network by the time he's twenty, become very rich and then die at the age of twenty-two.[17]

* * *

The average age among Neapolitan Camorra bosses is only thirty-five, while among the Casalesi clan and the 'Ndrangheta it is closer to fifty-five. In Naples there are no entry rules: a mere handbag snatcher can become a boss overnight. The absence of strict rules fragments the organization; more anarchic than its counterparts, it is all the more dangerous.[18] Such anarchy, which also holds sway in the rules of succession, allows women to seize power more easily than in other mafias.

One event marked a significant change within the Camorra: the Irpinia earthquake of 23 November 1980. At 7.34pm a main tremor of 6.9 on the Richter scale was felt across a wide area of southern Italy, followed by a succession of aftershocks. In all, some 3,000 deaths were recorded, with 8,000 injured and 300,000 people left homeless. International solidarity was mobilized, and more than 500 billion lire were sent to the affected area to help survivors. There was no question that the Camorra could overlook this vast sum and do nothing. It duly strengthened its ties with local politicians and succeeded in bidding for, and winning, public-sector contracts. For Amato Lamberti, director of the Osservatorio sulla Camorra,[19] the *camorristi* quickly understood that the domain of public works could be as profitable as contraband tobacco or drug trafficking: 'Think of the context in the region in the aftermath of the earthquake. Everything had to be rebuilt, from roads to public and private buildings ... The Camorra was offering its men, its heavy plant machinery, its businesses. Thanks to its ties to the corrupt political class, it managed to make a clean sweep of the bidding competitions and became a real partner in the reconstruction process.'[20] Many years later, however, tens of thousands of people were still living in makeshift shanties: the reconstruction projects were never completed and the funds were misappropriated.

The Camorra's hour of glory still came, at the end of the 1980s, when after the drug trade and the earthquake it discovered the juiciest of all business opportunities: waste disposal. Rubbish became the real *oro di Napoli* (Naples gold) for the colossal fortunes that it allowed mafia families to accumulate. One such clan, the Casalesi, named after the inhabitants of Casal di Principe near Caserta, launched itself into the business; within a few years it had taken the place of the failing public service, which could no longer deal with the 7,500 tons of waste produced daily in the Neapolitan agglomeration. Once collected, the rubbish was tipped into dumps, 'wild' or 'legal', where environmental and public health regulations were often ignored.[21] From the mid-1990s this practice was expanded to include the illicit dumping of toxic waste. The result was devastating. A land that had been named by the Romans as *Campania Felix* (fertile country) was now described as 'the land of fires' or 'the triangle of death'. The pollution of both soil and water was such that the World Health Organization estimated an excess mortality of 12 per cent compared with the rest of Italy among those living within a kilometre of the clandestine dumps.

* * *

It is said that the Casalesi clan no longer exists today. The important families—Schiavone, Bidognetti and Iovine—are all in jail: fathers, their sons and even a number of women. And in 2014, to general amazement, the last major boss, Antonio Iovine, decided to collaborate with the authorities and reveal the secrets of his clan.

Yet Rosaria Capacchione, an anti-mafia journalist, remains cautious:

> As long as the factors that allowed the families to take power in the first place are not addressed, we can't stop five idiots from rebuilding a clan. The mentality has not changed, people are still willing to acknowledge a boss figure. There's a certain cultural backwardness, but also backwardness on the part of the state. In this part of the world today, it is

still helpful to be a *camorrista* or a friend of a *camorrista*. That gives you easy access to economic resources that you would otherwise never dare to dream about. It's all very well to arrest people, but what really needs to be smashed is the mechanism that makes it advantageous to be on the side of the *camorriste*.[22]

In Casal di Principe and the surrounding villages, the mafia is more entrepreneurial than in Naples, and women play no role in the organization's affairs. Their job is to take care of the house and make sure that children grow up with mafia 'values': those of revenge, a sense of honour and *omertà*. Between 1996 and 2005, thirty-seven women were arrested on charges of illegal mafia association in Campania: thirty-three were from Naples and only four from the surrounding region.[23]

There was one exception, however: Anna Mazza, nicknamed 'the widow Moccia' after her dead husband. She reigned for more than twenty years over the small town of Afragola in the suburbs of Naples. The Moccia family had formed an extremely powerful clan that had made a fortune in property development. The widow would not allow drug dealing in her fiefdom but she is thought to have been behind several murders and, for her own security, had a bodyguard comprised of women. Legend has it that her first armed exploit dated to the 1970s, when she provided her thirteen-year-old son with a weapon to kill her husband's alleged murderer, as at thirteen there is no risk of being sent to prison. She was eventually acquitted of the homicide charge due to insufficient evidence. Never in the history of Italian organized crime has there been such a powerful female figure.

In the region around Naples mafia men make no secret of having mistresses, but are severe in judging unfaithful wives. Carmine Schiavone, a former Casalesi clan boss turned informer, recalled during an interview, with his wife present: 'I had many mistresses, women liked me a great deal. I was an expert in the art of love! We men were allowed to cheat. On the other hand, if a women cheated on her husband she was either killed or rejected and thrown out of her family with dishonour.' In the Sicilian or Calabrian mafias, men conceal their mistresses, as betraying one's family is dishonourable and it is said that a man who cheats on his wife is a man without values who might also betray his clan. In Naples, however, mafiosi are open about their infidelities and their women accept it. Giuseppe Misso, a former boss of the Sanità district, has revealed that when he was in prison and his mistress was about to give birth, he asked his wife to be present on his behalf—which she was.[24]

In contrast with the countryside, in Naples itself women are equally free to have lovers and to divorce. Maria,[25] a dealer in one of the city's central working-class neighbourhoods since she was thirteen, admits that women from the mafia milieu frequently have lovers. Husbands are more often than not in prison, their wives are young, and the fact that they see other men is tolerated so long as they prove their loyalty by continuing to visit their husbands in jail. Maria lives in one of those narrow streets where washing hangs from every balcony and the music of popular Neapolitan singers, the *neomelodici*, wafts through the window. She lives there with her entire family, about sixty people, and they control one of the biggest marijuana dealing hotspots in the city centre.

Grandparents, parents, children and grandchildren, boys and girls—anybody who is not in prison—are involved. From the age of thirteen, children here have their first encounters with the police, for theft or drug dealing, since the Camorra needs all hands on deck to manage its various types of trafficking, and the whole family, including mistresses, is expected to pull its weight. It is not considered impolite when meeting women in the family to enquire how many of their children are in prison, as death and prison are simply part of their lives. These women are cheerful, willing and ready and, bizarrely, addicted to bingo, often spending all their money in the bingo halls that are found everywhere in Naples. Maria admits to sometimes losing as much as €1,000 in a single evening. Women are active not only in the drug trade but also in illicit lotto scams, moneylending and contraband.

There are dozens of places in Naples where dealers operate. Attilio P., a policeman in the city, has explained that every week women are arrested for selling drugs, and it is often they who run the business, marginalizing their husbands. On 11 April 2015, Patrizia Chiavarone, aged fifty-one and a cocaine dealer, was arrested at her home, where she lived with her invalid mother and her husband. Searching for drugs, the police finally located a stash of cocaine in the incontinence pad worn by the sick mother. 'The man clearly had no say in the whole matter.' As tradition dictated, members of the family congregated outside the police station to bid a final farewell to the relative being sent to prison. Chiavarone's elder sister, a *masculona* (a woman who 'looks like a man'), then assaulted several police officers and was also arrested.

The Neapolitan police and judiciary have always paid particular attention to women within the mafia milieu. As magistrate Giuseppe Narducci puts it, 'Whereas in the 'Ndrangheta we hardly know the names of the bosses' wives, in the Camorra in Naples we know them all.' When members of a clan in the city are arrested, the whole family is taken to the police station, including daughters, mothers and grandmothers. In January 2011 the authors were present when members of a very important mafia clan—the Mazzarella family from the Forcella district—were rounded up by police. The family had ruled over one of the most lucrative drug dealing locations in the city. Of the fourteen individuals taken into custody, five were women who took care of selling cocaine and keeping lookout for police. There was also the grandmother, aged sixty-five, who put the cocaine into wraps that she hid behind the toilet (to be quickly flushed away in the event of a police raid). She then put the wraps into a bucket that she would lower from her window whenever she received an order.

Women also have an important role to play when arrests are attempted, with the aim of obstructing the forces of law and order. In scenes of pure Neapolitan theatricality they will put themselves between police and the wanted individual, allowing the suspect more time to escape. In the cramped alleys of the city's poor districts women scream from their balconies and throw down soapy water or whatever comes to hand to make the police motorbikes skid and prevent them from reaching the suspect's front door. In June 2005 hundreds of women and children came out onto the Piazza Ottocalli to block the police who had just arrested a clan member. The same thing had occurred some five months earlier when Cosimo Di Lauro, one of the main chiefs of the powerful Secondigliano clan, faced arrest.

Far from the female stereotypes of submission and discretion, the Camorra's women are tough, strong-minded and refuse to be mere housewives. Described as such for centuries in Neapolitan literature, they marry, divorce, and have lovers; they are modern women who wear make-up, who follow fashion, who are invariably well groomed. Like Donna Imma, the boss' wife in the *Gomorra* TV series, with her high heels and printed fabrics, many conform to a Camorra type of uninhibited sexiness, in which women are often out of the house, talk loudly and are hard to ignore: '*Sono donne di guai!* (Those women are trouble!)' says Isaia Sales, professor of the history of mafias. And because of their sexual freedom they are also a source of wars between families, of murders and vendettas.

The Camorra is less macho than the other mafias and more tolerant, and Naples is the only place where transsexuals or gay people have operated as clan bosses—an unthinkable state of affairs in Casal di Principe or in Calabria.[26] The fact that Anna Terracciano, nicknamed '*o Masculone* (Butch), liked women did not prevent her from being accepted and respected in the city's central Spanish Quarters. She was arrested in 2006 for, among other things, grievous bodily harm inflicted on a young man from a rival clan.[27] In 1994, Angela Barra, the mistress of Francesco Bidognetti, an important Casalesi boss, became attracted to a female hairdresser. When the latter rejected her advances Barra had her kidnapped, locked in an apartment and raped by her brother. The young woman managed to escape several weeks later and told her boyfriend what had happened to her. As her punishment, Angela Barra ordered the murder of the young man, who was twenty-five.[28] Ketty, a *camorrista* from Scampia, the modern northern district made famous for drug dealing by *Gomorrah*, is transgender. Under his real name, Ugo Gabriele, the *femminiello*—part of a longstanding Neapolitan sub-culture of effeminacy—ran a drug dealing and prostitution business before his arrest in February 2009.[29]

* * *

In the chapters that follow we have chosen to look at the lives of five of the best-known Camorra women, all of whom have played major roles at the heart of the organization and all of whom are still alive today. We tried to meet them, but the Camorra holds its female affiliates to the fundamental principle of *omertà*. We tried to contact all of them via their lawyers, by knocking on their door, or even by Facebook, but none of them wanted to talk to us. We had to have these women 'tell their story' through magistrates, journalists, mafia specialists and their lawyers. Though we failed to meet them personally, we also spent time with women from their Neapolitan neighbourhoods and backgrounds to try to understand the world in which they grew up. But women from Casale or from the region around the city were no more willing to open the heavily guarded doors of their homes to us.

PART THREE: WOMEN IN THE CAMORRA

We will trace the life stories of Pupetta Maresca, who, aged twenty and six months pregnant, shot the man responsible for her husband's death at point blank range; Erminia 'Celeste' Giuliano, who took over the reins of the family clan after her brothers' arrests; Maria Licciardi, sister of a boss of the Secondigliano Alliance, based in a deprived Naples suburb, who took over the drug dealing and extortion businesses with an iron hand after her brother was jailed; and finally Giuseppina Nappa and Anna Carrino from the powerful Casalesi clan—the former remained faithful to her husband, while the latter chose to escape the mafia fold by informing and collaborating.

8

PUPETTA MARESCA

INSULTED HONOUR

The phenomenon of female emancipation through crime is older within the Neapolitan Camorra than in the mafias of Calabria and Sicily. The famous case of Pupetta Maresca, a member of the Nuova Famiglia, stretches back to the 1950s.

Assunta Maresca or *Pupetta*, 'little doll',[1] was born on 19 January 1935 in Castellammarre di Stabia, a town of about 65,000 inhabitants near Pompeii in the province of Naples. The daughter of Alberto Maresca, a *camorrista* specializing in cigarette trafficking, her family, comprising four brothers and a sister, were nicknamed the 'Lampetielli' (from *lampo*, lightning), for the speed with which they wielded a knife. Pupetta was no exception: at school she was accused of wounding another girl, who preferred to withdraw her accusations upon leaving hospital.[2]

Each year, on 8 May, the family gave thanks to Our Lady of Pompeii in memory of the day on which Alberto escaped from prison by lowering a sheet from a toilet window, and the date was celebrated with a lavish party with concert and fireworks.

Pupetta was known for her flamboyant looks, to the point where at nineteen she won the local 'Miss Rovigliano' beauty contest named after a *comune* near Naples. It was not long before she caught the attention of Pasquale Simonetti or 'Pasquale 'e Nola', a young *camorrista* working in Naples' fruit and vegetable market but also an illicit cigarette and contraband runner. He was the *presidente dei prezzi*, the 'president of prices' who fixed the prices of agricultural products—often through violent means[3]—controlled the supply from the countryside to the city's wholesale markets and selected the buyers.

The Lampetielli gave their blessing to the engagement on 8 May 1954, the saint's day of the Madonna of Pompeii, but there was one small obstacle in the way of the marriage itself: Pasquale had to serve a short prison sentence and Pupetta refused to marry him until he handed himself in to the police. When he came out of jail six months later they were married on 27 April 1955.[4] On the day of the ceremony they made the short journey to the Shrine of the Virgin of the Rosary of Pompeii, where Pasquale handed his revolver to his wife and solemnly promised that he would change his life.

He didn't have much time to keep his promise. Three months later, on 16 July, he was assassinated on the orders of a rival by Gaetano Orlando. Pupetta left for San Giovanni Rotondo, a city in Puglia very heavily influenced by the cult of Padre Pio,[5] and swore vengeance there. Three weeks later, on 4 August, a heavily pregnant Pupetta and her brother Ciro walked into the Gardone bar on Naples' Corso Novara near the city's central station; in broad daylight, with several shots fired from her Smith & Wesson 0.38, she killed the man who had ordered Pasquale's murder, Antonio Esposito.[6]

'This killing was very unusual,' says Camorra expert Isaia Sales. 'Pascalone was a very important figure. Pupetta could have sent hired killers to carry it out, but she didn't, because in her culture committing a crime is something that should be public. This is very different from the Sicilian mafia, which is more discreet. The Sicilian mafia is based on impunity: you're a mafioso if you succeed in avoiding arrest or if you're released once you've been arrested. That is proof of power. The mafioso seeks impunity and doesn't want witnesses. In the Camorra, on the contrary, to show your power you have to offer a public spectacle, to theatricalize violence: they favour a duel in front of everybody, or a public assassination. That is a crime of honour. Pupetta's act was totally novel, showing that she was putting herself on the same level as her husband, that she was taking his place.'[7]

For the journalist Clare Longrigg, who met her on several occasions between 1995 and 1996, 'Pupetta couldn't run the risk of her husband's death going unpunished, her reputation would have suffered and she would have been deprived of her status as the widow of an important mafioso. Pupetta Maresca, daughter of the Lampetielli clan, could not be a passive victim; she knew that she had to earn publicly her reputation as a woman of honour.'[8]

Pupetta was arrested a few weeks later, on 14 October 1955, and taken to Poggioreale prison where she was detained in the section used to accommodate expectant mothers. As the investigation into her case was starting she gave birth to her son, Pasquale Jnr, in prison, where she was to raise him until the age of three, when he was entrusted to his maternal grandmother. When Pupetta was eventually released from jail, her son called her 'Pupetta' and his grandmother 'mother'. It was a painful experience, which she recounted to Clare Longrigg in 1995: 'When he was three they took my son away. It was a terrible thing, the pain destroyed me. My son was afraid of everything because in prison he didn't see anything or anyone. That's why when he went outside he would scream every time a car went past ... What do you expect me to say about my son? I can't say anything, it's too painful.'[9]

Pupetta's trial opened in April 1959 in Naples' criminal court. Media interest was so intense that in the US *Time* and *The New*

York Times devoted several columns to developments in the trial.[10] For the first time in its history, the court authorized the use of microphones so that members of the public could follow the trial. Public opinion was passionate, torn between 'pupettisti', who viewed the murder as a crime of passion and Pupetta as a heroine, and 'anti-pupettisti', who believed that the murder was premeditated. Pupetta opted for a strategy of self-defence, declaring: 'I killed for love but also because they wanted to kill me! And if my husband came back to life and they killed him again, I would do the same thing'—a statement that was met with applause from around the courtroom.[11]

For the prosecuting magistrate, however, it was less a crime of passion than a murder linked to conflict between rival *camorristi*. Gaetano Orlando, the assassin ordered by Antonio Esposito to kill Pasquale Simonetti, was sentenced to thirty years' imprisonment, while Pupetta received a sentence of eighteen years with the mitigating circumstance of 'provocation'. Her brother Ciro, still a minor at the time of the killing, was sentenced to twelve years. On appeal, Pupetta's sentence was reduced to thirteen years and four months and Ciro was acquitted.

Maria (a pseudonym), a drug dealer from the age of fourteen, had her first spell in prison at nineteen and got to know Pupetta, who took her under her wing: 'She was a very charismatic woman. Everyone respected her in prison. She made all the decisions,' she recalled.[12] This impression was confirmed by Clare Longrigg: 'Pupetta was waited on in prison, she was brought hot coffee and clean bed linen. The women prisoners hovered around her, hoping to meet her, and sent her messages asking for her help: could she intercede on their behalf with the judge or the prison director? Could she do something for so-and-so who had problems? Pupetta became the prisoners' *boss*. She had food taken to the weakest and defended their rights.'[13]

Pupetta was finally pardoned and freed ten years later, on 17 April 1965.[14] She then tried to rebuild her life and, taking advantage of her celebrity status, played herself in the 1967 film *Delitto a Posillipo*, loosely based on her biography, before opening two clothes shops in Naples. In 1970, she seemingly found love with *camorrista* Umberto Ammaturo, a drug trafficking specialist, with whom she had twins, Roberto and Antonella, without ever agreeing to marry him. In the meantime, her older son Pasquale had followed in his father's footsteps by becoming a delinquent. One day in 1974, on his way to see his stepfather about 'a certain job' near the railway station, he was killed in an ambush: his body was never found. He had never accepted his mother's relationship with Ammaturo and threatened him on several occasions. Ammaturo was accused of Pasquale's death but released in 1975 due to insufficient evidence.

Pupetta, though, could not shake the idea that Ammaturo was responsible: 'I always thought that Pasqualino annoyed him, he was too much like his father. I think that if he'd confessed the murder to me I would have killed again, without hesitation.'[15] She would not denounce him to the authorities, however: their children, the good life she had as the 'first lady' of drug running and the financial security it brought were reasons enough to remain silent. But relations between Pupetta and Ammaturo were never the same again and in 1982 they separated. When, years later, in 1993, Ammaturo was arrested in Peru in the company of his rich and beautiful new fiancée Yohanna Valdez, Pupetta declared: 'For me Umberto no longer exists: he is just the father of my children, who love and respect him as they should.'

Pupetta was not a woman to scare easily, nor was she one to advocate discretion as required by mafia tradition. On 13 February 1982, at the height of the war between the Nuova Camorra Organizzata and the Nuova Famiglia, she organized a press conference attended not only by all the city's print journalists but also television crews, in what was the biggest ever such mafia-organized event. She did not hesitate to directly threaten Raffaele

Cutolo, the head of the NCO: 'If by *Nuova Famiglia* you mean people opposed to that man's excess of power, then I consider myself as belonging to this organization.' A journalist took offence: 'Signora, have you brought us here to pass on your messages to your enemies? We have rules here, and respect justice.' An undaunted Pupetta replied: 'Yes, but justice and I have never been great friends. You know, justice has always punished me more harshly than I've deserved. The other day I overhead a *carabiniere* in my town say, "They've killed one of ours" when talking about the murder of one of Cutolo's clan. Tell me, where is the justice in that?'[16]

Pupetta was soon to reap what she had sown. First she was accused, wrongly, by Raffaele Cutolo himself of the murder of one of his affiliates, Ciro Galli, in 1981—a charge of which she was eventually acquitted due to lack of evidence in 1985. Then, in 1982, she and Umberto Ammaturo were arrested on suspicion of organizing the murder of controversial psychiatrist and criminologist Aldo Semerari, who had declared Cutolo insane to get his sentence reduced. Semerari had previously helped Ammaturo and other Nuova Famiglia affiliates and allies with 'helpful' psychiatric diagnoses, but after he was seen to shift allegiance to the NCO his decapitated corpse was discovered in his car in Ottaviano, Cutolo's fiefdom. Ammaturo got off, but Pupetta spent four years in Bellizzi Irpino's prison, where it is said she held parties to which magistrates were invited,[17] before being released, again because of insufficient proof.[18]

Nevertheless, her memories of her imprisonment, which she blamed on the omnipotent Cutolo, were bitter: 'I was tortured every day of those four years by the magistrates who locked me up. The first ten years [1955–65] were different because I had committed murder and it was right that I should pay. But those four years were terrible, there's no peace for an innocent locked up in prison.'[19]

In 1986, despite her acquittal and release, Pupetta was still convicted of mafia association, namely of being a *camorrista* affiliated to the Nuova Famiglia. The Tribunal of Naples ordered the confiscation of her assets, including her two shops. In 2004, her apartment in Naples became the property of the town hall, used as an office for social services.[20]

Today Pupetta Maresca lives in Castellammare di Stabia, her hometown,[21] in an apartment on one of the main streets of this small Neapolitan suburb. We rang at the door, but Pupetta didn't answer. We were told that she was an elderly woman, that she no longer had all her wits about her. This was not the case: she spoke to us at length on the telephone, but she refused to meet us, as she did not want to be associated with women from the Camorra, of which, she insisted, she was not part. According to her, if she had killed, it was for the sake of love, and, she added, when she had spoken out her words had been twisted. She was, however, prepared to meet us on receipt of a handsome fee—proof, perhaps, that she still had some wits about her.

Pupetta's story has inspired filmmakers such as Francesco Rosi (*La Sfida*, 1958) and Marisa Malfatti and Riccardo Tortora (*Il caso Pupetta Maresca*, 1982). In 2013, Italy's Canale 5 channel broadcast a four-part mini-series entitled *Pupetta: Il coraggio e la passione*. Another film, produced by RAI, was only shown in its entirety in 1994 after a court in Rome ruled that it did not have to be cut as it did not damage Pupetta's reputation. She had taken legal action to stop the distribution of the film, which she described as 'a massacre. They've turned my life into a series of idiocies ... Everybody knows about my personal tragedy ... I killed for love, not to act out some scene. I was nineteen years old and Pasqualone was the love of my life ... We were married for eighty days, no longer than a sigh and then ... they killed him and I lost everything: innocence, youth, passion ... Now I would just like some peace.'[22]

This tirade was put into context by Clare Longrigg's description of Pupetta's personality: 'During our conversations she never gave me the impression of a person tortured by pain. Even I—and I am generally very emotional and break down in tears at stories of loved ones strangled and dissolved in acid—felt strangely indifferent towards her story. She is a completely cold person. Beautiful and glacial.'[23]

9

ERMINIA GIULIANO

'LADY CAMORRA'

'This woman is a leader. She has qualities normally reserved for men: charisma and organizational ability.' This is how the head of the *carabinieri*, hunting her down, described Erminia Giuliano.[1]

Erminia's destiny was determined by her birthplace, Forcella, a poor but vibrant district in the shadow of Naples' Duomo. In this labyrinth of alleys, under a rainbow of washing hanging from balconies, scooters whizz by while women shout out of their windows. 'It's said that you find the most beautiful women in Naples in this neighbourhood. But they also have a reputation for being the loudest and the most exuberant: they're modern and entrepreneurial women for whom sex plays an important role,' explains Giuseppe Narducci, magistrate at the city's public prosecutor's office.[2]

Forcella is inextricably linked with the Giuliano family, one of the city's most powerful Camorra clans. The name Giuliano does not merely stand for a family and a district, but it evokes a whole era: the 1970s and 1980s, important years for Naples which saw

Diego Maradona gift the city the title of national champions, and the famous *Scudetto* (champions' shield), on 10 May 1987. Today Maradona, the footballing genius, is still venerated by Neapolitans who have elevated him almost to the status of the city's patron saint. His image can be found everywhere in bars and alleyways, side by side with Padre Pio and the Virgin Mary.[3]

The notoriety of this dynasty was due to its legendary chief, Luigi Giuliano, father of eleven children. Several of these, notably Pio Vittorio, succumbed to the siren calls of organized criminality, moving in the course of the 1970s from contraband cigarettes to kidnappings, protection rackets and pimping. It was such a spectacular rise that in a famous photo from the late 1980s Diego Maradona is seen proudly clinking champagne glasses with Erminia Giuliano.

Pio Vittorio Giuliano himself also had eleven children, six boys (Luigi, Guglielmo, Nunzio, Carmine, Salvatore and Raffaele) and five girls (Erminia, Anna, Patrizia, Silvana and Antonietta), said to be very beautiful, tough and independent. Their amorous escapades and infidelities were notorious common knowledge, not least because they would sleep with magistrates and senior police officers to buy their favour. Luigi, the oldest, nicknamed *'O Re*, the King, became head of the clan. A singer and part-time lyricist, he organized numerous parties and concerts for Forcella's residents, who liked and respected him. 'He invented the Totocalcio [football pools] and the clandestine street lotto, and he enjoyed extraordinary public support,' says Giuseppe Narducci. Then there was Raffaele, the youngest of the clan, who threw his wife from a third-floor balcony after excessive cocaine consumption. Arrested, he was the first in the family to collaborate with the authorities, followed by Guglielmo, Carmine and even 'the King' himself.

With no men left, the Giuliano clan was effectively decapitated and broken. Or so it seemed until Erminia took control with an iron fist. Rosaria Capacchione, a well-known Neapolitan journalist and politician who has been threatened by the Camorra, tells this story:

> One day I was on a bus in Naples on the route that goes from the station to the Piazza del Plebiscito. It was full to bursting point, you could hardly breathe, and as for sitting down I'll let you imagine! The bus pulled over to a stop and a young woman got on, very beautiful and covered in jewels. On a bus in Naples! That just doesn't happen. She got on with two other people and then suddenly everybody started making room for her. I don't even know how they managed to make space but miraculously a seat became free and after she sat down they continued to leave some space around her. That can give you an idea of what Erminia was like.[4]

Beautiful and nonconformist, she was nicknamed Celeste after her bright blue eyes, and Bionda, blonde, because of her stylish hair. She collected both lovers and leopard-print outfits. But she had also always been the family's expert in managing property assets and money invested in the commercial sector. Even when her brothers were still at the head of the clan, Erminia was already independently running the moneylending and—according to later investigations—the extortion sides of the business.[5] Above all, she was more than willing to engage in intimate relations with the enemy camp: after she separated from her husband Giuseppe Roberti, she started an affair with Patrizio Bosti of the rival Contini clan. According to her informer brother Luigi's statements, this relationship led to her involvement in the murder of Vincenzo Avigliano, a friend and associate of Luigi.[6] Just at the moment when the Giuliano family seemed to be shattered by vendettas, murders and informers, Erminia was to become increasingly involved in its criminal activities.

Through determination and charisma, she managed to rebuild clan networks, gambling on those affiliates still at large and on younger generations: sons, nephews and sons-in-law acquired through cunning matrimonial strategies.[7] Her reputation as a tenacious woman was complemented by her readiness to take direct action, as on the day in 1997 when she stabbed a female rival or two years later, when she deliberately drove her car into the window of a toy shop whose owner had refused to pay the *pizzo*, the protection money traditionally extorted from shop-keepers. She was soon to appear on a list drawn up by the authorities of Italy's thirty most wanted criminals.[8]

On 23 December 2000, Lady Camorra was finally apprehended by police after a ten-month hunt in the *vicoli*, the city's maze of alleys. She was only hiding in the Forcella district, at her daughter's home, concealed behind a sliding panel attached to a bedroom wall like a true 'Ndrangheta boss reluctant to lose control of his territory. She seemed unmoved when the handcuffs were put on and merely said, 'Let me get my hair done' before phoning her hairdresser to come to the apartment. Then, clad in leopard-print coat and high heels, she said, 'I'm all yours' and was taken to the prison in Rebibbia, in the eastern suburbs of Rome. On 20 April 2006, she was sentenced to ten years' imprisonment for 'participation in the Giuliano *camorrista* organization' with the aggravating circumstance of having 'organized and directed that criminal association'.[9]

The authorities seized more than €28 million in assets belonging to the family, including property companies and fashion outlets, the financial lifeblood of the clan.[10] Was this the end of an era? It would appear likely that Erminia's daughters, Gemma and Milena, have followed in their mother's footsteps. In 1993, Nicola Gatti, aged seventeen, was murdered and thrown in the sea, weighed down by an anchor, off the island of Ischia. Rumour had it that he had slept with both sisters.

10

MARIA LICCIARDI

'THE GODMOTHER'

Maria Licciardi, head of the powerful Secondigliano clan, named after a modern suburb to the north of Naples, was asleep in prison when her husband Antonio Teghemié was arrested by police in the summer of 2005 for a minor crime. The headline in the next day's *Il Mattino* was explicit: 'Boss' husband arrested'.[1]

Born in Secondigliano on 24 March 1951, Maria was heiress to an important dynasty of Camorra chiefs or *guappi*. She was the sister of Pietro, Vincenzo and Gennaro Licciardi, the last nicknamed *'a Scigna* ('the Monkey') and a founding member of the *Alleanza de Secondigliano* (the Secondigliano Alliance), a coalition of formidable Camorra families controlling extortion rackets and drug dealing in several of Naples' suburbs.

Known as *'a Piccirella*, 'the Little One', on account of her slight stature, or the *Madrina*, 'the Godmother', Maria became the uncontested boss of the clan after the successive arrests of her brothers and husband in the early 1990s. Under her reign, the Secondigliano Alliance managed to extend its influence not only in drug dealing but also in the illicit cigarette market and—as a novelty—prostitution.

Responsible for several murders, Maria also had the particularly delicate task of convincing *camorristi* on the verge of collaborating with the authorities to change their minds in return for remuneration. In 1998, she was arrested in her car as she was about to hand 300 million lire (approximately €150,000) to Costantino Sarno, the number one contraband cigarette dealer, so that he would retract his statements. In detention he had previously expressed willingness to inform and collaborate.[2]

Reputedly cold, yet charismatic, Maria was highly gifted in business matters. According to Barbara Sargenti, prosecutor in the Naples Antimafia District Directorate, she was 'the woman who best exemplified the gender revolution within the Camorra. She was one of the best criminal brains inside the Secondigliano Alliance, where she managed all types of trafficking. She was a bloodthirsty woman, but also extremely strategic in her thinking. Not one of the informers who agreed to provide witness evidence on the activities of the mafia was able to point to the slightest crime that she might have committed, not even a case of extortion or witness intimidation.'[3] The journalist Lucia Licciardi (no relation) remarks: 'She behaves just like the head of a multinational. She always looks for a solution that's less likely to attract police attention and that creates fewer splits within the clan.'[4] According to the judge Luigi Bobbio, 'When a woman is at the head of a criminal organization, it is paradoxically possible to note a lesser degree of emotional involvement and better performances within the group.'[5]

When questioned in court about Maria Licciardi's role, and more generally about that of women in the Secondigliano Alliance, the *pentito* Gaetano Guida replied:

> They're at the forefront ... women (the wives, sisters and mothers of the bosses) have always been influential in decision-making. Maria Licciardi, Gennaro's sister, is a typical example. She would take orders and pass them on to her brother. She also delivered the important messages from

her brother, including orders to kill ... In our clan, speaking to Maria Licciardi was exactly the same thing as speaking to Gennaro, the boss. I can add that women carried out all sorts of tasks on behalf of the Alliance: they carried messages to prisoners, distributed money to members, organized the extortion rackets. In other words, they form the backbone of the organization.[6]

'The Godmother''s rise was spectacular during the 1990s, but her reign came to an abrupt end in 1999. That year a sizeable cargo of pure heroin from Istanbul was delivered to the port of Naples. Maria felt that the merchandise should not be sold in its unadulterated state as it risked killing the Alliance's clients. Disobeying her orders, members of the Lo Russo clan distributed the heroin on the streets, leading to the death of eleven people in April 1999 and increased police pressure on the Camorra. The Secondigliano Alliance split apart, four members of the Licciardi clan were killed and Maria led the inevitable counterattack. It was at this point that investigators learned of her existence.[7]

Joining the list of Italy's thirty most wanted criminals, she succeeded in evading capture for two years without ever leaving her stronghold of Masseria Cardone. From her hiding place she continued to direct her clan and may have ordered several assassinations.[8] She was finally arrested on 14 June 2001 in Melito di Napoli, a suburb of Naples, along with a couple: the man, accused of criminal complicity, was arrested, his wife released. First imprisoned in L'Aquila, she was transferred following the earthquake of 6 April 2009 to Rebibbia, where she was held under Article 41-bis of the Italian penal code, the strict legal regime reserved for the most prominent mafia bosses.[9]

11

GIUSEPPINA NAPPA

FAITHFUL TO 'SANDOKAN'

Giuseppina Nappa was the wife of Francesco Schiavone, nick-named 'Sandokan' for his resemblance to the pirate character in a popular television series. Notorious for both cruelty and gener-osity, he was a portrait painter in his spare time and capable of outwitting the police and legal system. Operating on an equal footing with local politicians, he was a remarkable businessman, 'the Toto Riina of the Camorra', with his clan's annual turnover estimated at some US$3 billion.[1]

Born into a very poor family, in the 1980s Schiavone rose through the ranks of the Bardellino clan, a powerful part of the Nuova Famiglia coalition in the north of Campania. After years of schisms and internecine murders he rose to become boss in the 1990s, and despite his modest background he was comfort-able in the company of politicians—his speciality was skimming public contracts and construction corruption in areas such as motorways as well as illicit waste management. After the devasta-tion of the 1980 earthquake, he and his clan siphoned off billions of lire destined for reconstruction in the region.

In 1990, Schiavone was arrested at the home of a local councillor, but three years later he took advantage of temporary leave from prison and disappeared. The legend of Sandokan grew spectacularly, and the fugitive was spotted everywhere.[2] He was only found and arrested after five years on the run when the police discovered him at home, in his fiefdom of Casal di Principe; the authorities had tracked him down by following his wife Giuseppina. After seven months of tailing her the police were convinced that Sandokan was inside a villa protected by a high wall in the very centre of town. Forty officers assaulted the building, but in what looked like a fiasco the villa was found empty. Even so, the police were sure that Schiavone was nearby and began probing the walls of the villa and garage, firing tear gas into pipes and cavities, but nothing was happening. After thirteen hours of searching they attacked a garage wall with a pneumatic drill. A few seconds later, they heard a voice behind the rubble shout out, 'I'm giving myself up, don't shoot, my children are with me.' In a cloud of tear gas, they found Sandokan, his wife, two of their children aged two and three, and an accomplice. The boss' hiding place was a luxurious four-floor apartment, accessed though a secret entrance in the best traditions of gothic melodrama.[3]

Giuseppina Nappa met Schiavone when she was still very young, as often happens with women in this region. She fell very much in love with him and they had seven children, whom she raised on her own. Her husband spent most of his time on the run and since 1998 has been locked up in the high security wing of an Italian prison. Yet Giuseppina did not fail to transmit his cultural and moral values to the children, steering them towards a life of crime based on the main key principles of making oneself respected and respecting a father's teachings. Weapons were left lying around the house, and in photographs of a family picnic pistols are clearly visible amongst the leftovers from the meal.

GIUSEPPINA NAPPA: FAITHFUL TO 'SANDOKAN'

During the years on the run and in hiding, Giuseppina knew that she had to take every precaution; her husband was viewed as one of Italy's most dangerous criminals and police across the country were looking for him. Always cautious, when travelling she would change vehicle several times and always take different routes. She was the perfect mafia boss' wife: discreet, devoted to her husband and completely faithful, whereas her spouse accumulated extra-conjugal relationships, including one with a female British NATO operative.[4]

Giuseppina idolized this man, who in return offered her a life of hiding, prison and death. Rosaria Capacchione, an anti-mafia journalist living under protection, is familiar with the history of the Casalesi clans, who have ordered her death. She has described how Sandokan's sons are all an exact copy of their father: 'They have the same beard as their father and the same sort of glasses. They worship him. This father who is jailed for life … Giuseppina sees her children copying their father and does nothing to stop it! Can you imagine? Any other mother would have reacted and told them: "Haven't you learnt from your father's mistakes?" It's as if power, money, being able to give orders, social status … all of these are stronger than love of the family. Even for women. Sandokan's wife has always wanted to remain Sandokan's wife.'

Giuseppina could have changed her life, and her husband suggested she should. When he was arrested in 1998 and realized that he would never leave prison again, he encouraged his wife to take the children away and to live with one of her sisters, a teacher of Italian. But she refused, thus condemning her sons to prison or death and her daughters to widowhood. Because who, other than a *camorrista*, would go out with one of Sandokan's daughters?

All their sons were arrested one after the other. 'I think that when they arrested Ivanhoe, her favourite, she saw the error of her ways … When the prison doors closed behind him she screamed out his name. But it was too late. He had been brought in for murder. She was the one who had passed on those values, because Ivanhoe was only seventeen years old when his father was sentenced. She was the one responsible for his education. Since his incarceration she is thought to have attempted suicide on several occasions,' says Capacchione.[5]

And yet Giuseppina Nappa is a regular at Mass in her home village of Casal di Principe. She is not impressed by anti-Camorra sermons and is keen to let that be known. In 2011 Don Carlo, priest at Casal, reported that after one of his homilies against the Camorra, Giuseppina appeared in his sacristy and announced, 'Don Carlo, I didn't like your preaching at all!' before walking out.[6]

Today, in her late fifties, Giuseppina is condemned to see her husband and son only once a month through the glass screen of a prison visiting room. In July 2002, her mother-in-law died, aged eighty-five, in the house they shared with those of the clan who are not in jail. Sandokan and his sons requested special leave to pay their respects—the magistrates refused.

* * *

Giuseppina, too, has chosen to die without ever really seeing the men of her family. But Walter, Sandokan's brother, married another sort of woman, one who did not want her children to choose a life of crime. Walter has been sentenced to life imprisonment, but his children have had no trouble with the law, living normal and unremarkable lives. They owe their destiny, very different from that of their cousins, to their mother's choice to bring them up far from the Camorra's school of crime.

12

ANNA CARRINO

THE WOMAN WHO SCARED THE CASALESI CLAN

'I got to know Francesco when I was thirteen. I thought he was my Prince Charming.'[1] So says Anna Carrino, partner of twenty-seven years of Francesco Bidognetti, the famous boss of the Casalesi clan,[2] and mother of his three children: Katia, Teresa and Gianluca.[3] He is fifteen years older than her.[4]

Giuseppe Narducci, the Naples-based anti-mafia magistrate, recalls:

Anna Carrino was Neapolitan, and she didn't come from a mafia family. She became [Bidognetti's] partner after the death of his first wife. She was certainly attracted to this man for his charisma and his strong personality. She was at the age where one is quite naïve and she must also have been drawn to the money, a factor that shouldn't be underestimated. Anna came from a humble background and Bidognetti earned a lot of money inside the organization. He was able to provide her with a house and material comfort. When Anna went out into the streets of Casal she was highly respected. Not because of what she was, but because she was the boss' partner.

When in 1993 Bidognetti was arrested and imprisoned under the Article 41-bis regime, Anna took over the leadership of the clan: she actively participated in the acquisition of assets and the management of Bidognetti's patrimonial interests by acting as his figurehead; she directly ran the extortion business and played a part in defining the clan's criminal strategy.[5] Above all, she worked as Bidognetti's messenger, and was the only person capable of decrypting his coded *pizzini*, the messages passed as gestures through the visiting room screen whose meaning was so complex that magistrates, despite video recordings, could never decipher them—until Anna gave them the clues they needed.

In the course of thirty years spent in Casal di Principe, the Casalesi stronghold, she welcomed the clan's highest dignitaries into her home, including Giuseppe Setola, a member of the Casalesi group's most murderous branch, and Luigi Guida, Bidognetti's right hand man. It was to Guida that she turned when one day in 2002 her young son Gianluca, known as Nanà, told her that Antonio Petito, a twenty-year-old carpenter, had tried to run him over as he was crossing the road. What for Petito had only been a lapse of concentration was a terrible affront for the Bidognetti family, and this was enough to dispatch a clan commando to kill the young driver.[6]

According to Giuseppe Narducci, 'Anna Carrino was a strong and arrogant woman, and she must have known that she was putting that young man in danger. Perhaps she didn't want him killed, but she knew that she was putting him at risk. At her trial it was judged that she was aware of this, and she was found guilty of the boy's murder.'

That same year she discovered that her husband had been unfaithful to her for twenty years[7] with Angela Barra, who headed the Teverola clan in Caserte province.[8] 'My world collapsed,' she confided to the journalist Flaminia Giambalvo. 'It was his lawyer who confirmed it was true, he hadn't had the courage to tell me to my face. A woman Francesco had had three more children with and who everybody knew about, including my sisters.'[9]

Her loyalty towards the clan now began to waver, until on 8 November 2007 she decided to leave Casal de Principe for good. 'I had my back to the wall. In 2007 they'd started arresting everyone, and I knew they'd end up getting me too. But it wasn't just because of this that I decided to collaborate. My family situation had become unbearable. My older daughter Katia had taken over and wanted her husband, Giovanni Lubello, to become Francesco's new intermediary. They wanted me out of the way at any cost. They wrote to Francesco telling him that I'd gone mad, that I was never at home, that I was in a bad way. These are hurtful things.'[10]

She then left for Rome, where she was detained a few days later, on 11 November, by the Direzione Investigativa Antimafia (DIA).[11] She quickly decided to collaborate with the authorities, becoming the first woman to inform on the redoubtable Casalesi clan. Giuseppe Narducci recalls: 'When she started to collaborate, I had a broken woman in front of me. It took courage to escape from the prison that Casal di Principe had become for her, and she had lost her bearings. Not one of her children wanted to follow her. That was the hardest moment in the collaboration process. She hoped that the youngest daughter would come with her. She was seventeen, but she didn't want to. They all took the father's side. She's a woman who suffered a terrible heartbreak.'

Rosaria Capacchione draws a similar picture:

When Anna Carrino became a *pentita* and informer she also became *schifosa*, 'repugnant'. Her children didn't just disown her officially, they did so in their hearts. They never wanted to see her again. As for their father, they had really only known him from prison visits [as he had been in jail since 1993]. But the children preferred to take his side. There's a very developed sense of family here. Their mother was the one who had abandoned the family. Anna Carino was born in Naples, in another culture. But she was never his wife ... because they never got married. And in these villages things like that matter. He had been married to his wife, that's all, and then she died and he never remarried.

Thanks to Anna's revelations, fifty-two affiliates of the clan were rounded up in April 2008, including one of Francesco Bidognetti's sons, Raffaele. In the months following her testimony, dozens more Casalesi clan members opted to collaborate, perhaps heralding the organization's decline.[12]

But in the mafia, betrayal calls for bloody reprisals. In May 2008, Gianluca, Anna's son, tried to kill his aunt and his cousin;[13] Anna herself, by this point dubbed a *superpentita* by the media, was then directly targeted in an assassination attempt by the clan.[14]

* * *

Today Anna Carrino lives under protection, in constant fear of being killed. She learned some years ago that her youngest daughter Teresa had given birth to a son, but she will not be able to hold her grandson in her arms. The laws of a life under protection prevent it, and this is a price that Anna has accepted she must pay.[15]

CONCLUSION

THE 'PSEUDO-EMANCIPATION' OF WOMEN

Women and the mafia: these terms have long been considered contradictory, evoking notions of vulnerability on the one hand and violence on the other. It is due to this well-established stereotype that the role of women in mafia organizations has been underestimated, if not ignored, in legal investigations and publications concerned with organized criminality. The predominant idea was of a submissive female, denied individuality and incapable of attaining any autonomy from her husband. Yet, as we have seen throughout this book, women have not only always played an essential part in the transmission of mafia values, but have also assumed a decisive role in the history of the familial clan, whether by choosing to take command when a boss was imprisoned, or by deciding to leave through collaboration with the authorities.

In the first instance, as exemplified by Giusy Vitale or Erminia Giuliano, rather than freeing themselves from the yoke of male domination, mafia women substituted themselves for men, identifying completely with the negative values that they had always known. Is it possible in such cases to talk of women's emancipation?

According to the American sociologist Freda Adler, a link exists between such emancipation and female criminality. She believes that if crime has always been the prerogative of men it is because of the sexual inequality that prevails in society and enshrines male superiority. The growing number of women accused of illegal mafia association, supported by statistics, therefore seems to point to a movement of female liberation. Yet for the Palermo prosecuting magistrate, Teresa Principato, it is impossible to view this phenomenon as anything more than 'pseudo-emancipation' and certainly not as liberation.

True liberation is perhaps to be found in the examples of women like Lea Garofalo or Anna Carrino, who chose to change their lives by turning themselves in, thereby cutting off the transmission of mafia (anti-)values that are often deeply rooted in a code of machismo.

NOTES

INTRODUCTION

1. *Encyclopædia Universalis*, vol. 14, 1992, p. 239.
2. John Dickie, *Cosa Nostra: A History of the Sicilian Mafia*, London: Hodder, 2007.

PART ONE: WOMEN IN COSA NOSTRA

1. John Dickie, *Cosa Nostra: A History of the Sicilian Mafia*, London: Hodder, 2007.
2. Attilio Bolzoni, *Parole d'onore*, Milan: Rizzoli, 2008.
3. Gadh Charbit and Anne Véron, interview with Gaspare Mutolo, April 2014.
4. *Capo* of Cinisi and one of the most important Cosa Nostra bosses of the 1970s.
5. Gaspare Mutolo and Anna Vinci, *La Mafia non lascia tempo*, Milan: Rizzoli, 2013.
6. A famous mafia family name from Acquasanta, a Palermo neighbourhood.
7. The basic unit of Cosa Nostra, the family.
8. Dickie, op. cit.
9. A *lupara* is a typical long shotgun, used by the Sicilian Mafia.
10. Gadh Charbit and Anne Véron, interview with Saverio Lodato, antimafia journalist, April 2014.
11. Gadh Charbit and Anne Véron, interview with Alessandra Dino, sociologist and mafia specialist, April 2014.

12. Interview with Gaspare Mutolo, op. cit.

13. Gadh Charbit and Anne Véron, *Corleone, la guerre des parrains*, TV documentary, 2014.

14. Interview with Gaspare Mutolo, *op. cit.*

15. Corleone is a small town, some 50 kilometres from Palermo; it has long been a mafia hotspot.

16. Anne Véron, interview with Letizia Battaglia, in *Des femmes dans la Mafia*, TV documentary, 2012.

17. Ibid.

18. Gadh Charbit and Anne Véron, *Le maxiprocès de la Mafia*, TV documentary, 2013.

19. Gadh Charbit and Anne Véron, interview with Giuseppe Ayala, September 2013.

20. Gadh Charbit and Anne Véron, interview with Alfonso Giordano, June 2013.

21. Anne Véron, interview with Maurizio De Lucia, anti-mafia magistrate, April 2012.

22. Gadh Charbit and Anne Véron, op. cit.

23. Gadh Charbit and Anne Véron, interview with Leonardo Guarnotto, July 2014.

24. Gadh Charbit and Anne Véron, interview with Vittorio Teresi, July 2014.

25. Ibid.

26. Interview with Leonardo Guarnotto, op. cit.

27. 'L'altra metà della Cupola' [The Other Half of the Cupola], *Revue Narcomafie*, October 2005.

28. Marcelle Padovani, *Mafia, mafias*, Paris: Découvertes Gallimard, 2009.

1. NINETTA BAGARELLA: WIFE OF THE 'BUTCHER OF CORLEONE'

1. Anne Véron, interview with Maurizio De Lucia, anti-mafia magistrate, April 2012.

2. Ibid.

3. Anne Véron, interview with Attilio Bolzoni, April 2012.

4. Anne Véron, interview with Pino Maniaci, April 2012.

5. Paola Bellone, Biography of Ninetta Bagarella, 'Cinquanta mila giorni, la Storia raccontata da Giorgio dell'Atri', *Corriere della Sera*, 24 March 2014.

6. Ibid.

7. Enrico Bellavia, 'Il racconto di Santino Di Matteo "Quando Brusca ordinò di uccidere mio figlio"', *La Repubblica*, 23 November 2010.

8. Toto Riina was born on 30 November 1930.

9. Mario Francese, 'Io mafiosa? Sono solo una donna innamorata' [Me, a mafiosa? I'm simply a woman in love], *Giornale della Sicilia*, 27 July 1971.

10. http://archiviopiolatorre.camera.it/img-repo/DOCUMENTAZIONE/Antimafia/04_rel_02.pdf

11. The equivalent of France's Ecoles Supérieures du Professorat et de l'Education (ESPE) or UCAS teacher training establishments in the UK.

12. Francesco Viviano and Alessandra Ziniti, 'Viaggi a Venezia, estate al mare, la dolce vita del latitante Riina' [Trips to Venice, summers by the sea, the *dolce vita* of the fugitive Riina], *La Repubblica*, 27 October 2014.

13. Letter published in *La Repubblica*, 23 June 1996.

14. 'Termini scaduti, libero Riina jr. E nasce la polemica: "Assurdo' [Riina junior freed, the controversy starts], *La Repubblica*, 28 February 2008.

15. 'Ergastolo per il figlio di Toto Riina' [Life sentence for the son of Toto Riina], *La Repubblica*, 23 November 2001.

16. Anne Véron, interview with Letizia Battaglia, in *Des femmes dans la Mafia*, TV documentary, 2012.

17. Anne Véron, interview with Alessandra Camassa, April 2012.

18. Reuters, 5 January 2008. http://it.reuters.com/article/topNews/idITPAR55334320080106

19. Attilio Bolzoni, 'La mia vita con un padre che si chiama Totò Riina' [My life with a father called Toto Riina], *La Repubblica*, 28 January 2009.

20. 'La fille de Toto Riina accorde sa première interview TV à la RTS' [Toto Riina's daughter gives her first interview to RTS], RTS, 26 August 2013.

21. Siana Vanella, 'La figlia di Riina: vi sembro donna di mafia?' [Riina's daughter: do you think I look like a mafiosa?], *Panorama*, 4 February 2014.

22. Lirio Abbate, 'Mafia, le relazioni pugliesi della moglie di Totò Riina' [Mafia, the Puglian links of Toto Riina's wife], *L'Espresso*, 23 January 2014.

2. RITA ATRIA: THE YOUNG REBEL

1. Graziella Proto, 'Rita Atria: Racconto tutto a Paolo Borsellino' [Rita Atria: I told everything to Paolo Borsellino], *ANTIMAFIADuemila*, 25 July 2012.

2. Petra Reski, 'Rita Atria, la picciridda dell'antimafia' [Rita Atria, the little anti-mafiosa], *Nuovi Mondi*, 2011.

3. Marcelle Padovani, *Mafia, mafias*, Paris: Découvertes Gallimard, 2009.

4. Anne Véron, interview with Michele Tamuzza, resident of Partanna and member of the Associazone Antimafia Rita Atria.

5. A state witness is an individual with no criminal past, who has seen or heard a criminal event or action and can testify as to its veracity in a court of law. He/she is entitled to protection and financial support from the state. The status of a state witness is defined in Italy by Law No. 45/2001 of 2001.

6. A *collaboratore di giustizia*, a 'justice collaborator', is an individual who has taken part in criminal activities and who agrees to cooperate with the police and legal authorities, in return for certain benefits (sentence reduction, protection and financial aid).

7. Véron, interview with Michele Tamuzza, op. cit.

8. http://www.ritaatria.it/Testimoni/RitaAtria/IlDiario.aspx

9. Reski, op. cit.

10. Anne Véron, interview with Alessandra Camassa, April 2012.

11. Reski, op. cit.

12. Founded in 1980, the Women Against the Mafia committee became the Association of Sicilian Women Against the Mafia in 1984. Composed exclusively of women, most of whose families are Mafia victims, the organization's objective is to denounce complicity and to break silence on the Mafia's practices. It supports women who bring civil

proceedings against the Mafia in court. At the time of writing, the Association had suspended its activities.

13. A group of women who started to meet in 1992 at Palermo's Piazza Castelnuovo after the murders of Falcone and Borsellino. Le donne del digiuno, to fast in order to denounce the Mafia and demonstrate their 'hunger for justice'.

14. Anne Véron, interview with Letizia Battaglia, in *Des femmes dans la Mafia*, TV documentary, 2012.

15. 'Un affronto a Rita, pentita suicida' [An affront to Rita, the *pentita* who committed suicide], *Corriere della Sera*, 22 November 1992.

16. Alessandra Zitini, 'Condannata a 2 mesi la madre di Rita Atria' [Rita Atria's mother sentenced to 2 months in prison], *La Repubblica*, 13 October 1993.

3. GIUSY VITALE: THE FIRST 'GODMOTHER' OF COSA NOSTRA

1. Giusy Vitale with Camilla Costanzo, *Ero cosa loro, l'amore di una madre puo sconfiggere la mafia* [I Was Their Thing: A mother's love can defeat the mafia], Milan: Arnoldo Mondadori Editore, 2009.

2. Definition from www.garzantilinguistica.it (accessed 25 November 2016).

3. Vitale with Costanzo, op. cit.

4. Anne Véron, interview with Alessandra Dino, April 2012.

5. Anne Véron, interview with Pino Maniaci, April 2012.

6. Alessandra Dino, interview with Giusy Vitale, 8 May 2009.

7. Véron, interview with Alessandra Dino, op. cit.

8. Anne Véron, interview with Maurizio De Lucia, anti-mafia magistrate, April 2012.

9. Marcelle Padovani, 'Mafia: un boss en jupons' [Mafia: a boss in petticoats], *Le Nouvel Observateur*, 25 August 2005.

10. Vitale with Costanzo, op. cit.

4. CARMELA IUCULANO: FOR THE LOVE OF HER CHILDREN

1. Carla Cerati, *Storia vera di Carmela Iuculano, la giovane donna che si è*

ribellata a un clan mafioso [The real story of Carmela Iuculano, the young woman who rebelled against a mafia clan], Venice: Marsilio, 2009.

2. Carmela Iuculano, testimony given at the Tribunal of Palermo, 13 March 2006.

3. RAI Educational, *La Storia siamo noi, Donne di mafia: l'urlo e il silenzio* [History, it's us, Mafia women: the cry and the silence], TV documentary, 2007.

4. Ibid.

5. Cerati, op. cit.; Iuculano, op. cit.

6. Cerati, op. cit.

7. Anne Véron, interview with Carmela Iuculano, 6 November 2014.

8. Ibid.

9. Ibid.

10. Cerati, op. cit.

11. Véron, interview with Carmela Iuculano, op. cit.

12. Ibid.

13. Cerati, op. cit.

14. Iuculano, op. cit.

PART TWO: WOMEN IN THE 'NDRANGHETA

1. Marcelle Padovani, *Mafia, mafias*, Paris: Découvertes Gallimard, 2009.

2. Kahina Sekkai, 'John Paul Getty III, la mort d'un héritier' [John Paul Getty III, the death of an heir], *Paris Match*, 11 February 2011.

3. Anne Véron, interview with Giuseppe Baldessarro, journalist specializing in the 'Ndrangheta for *La Repubblica*, July 2013.

4. According to the Italian social research organization Eurispes, http://www.eurispes.eu/content/ndrangheta-holding-dossier-2008

5. Tristan Dessert, 'Sur les traces de la 'Ndrangheta, la plus puissante des mafias d'Italie' [On the trail of the 'Ndrangheta, the most powerful of Italy's mafias], France 24 report, 21 May 2013.

6. Padovani, op. cit.

7. 'Bien implantés à Milan' [Solidly rooted in Milan], article from *L'Eco di Bergamo* published in special edition of *Courrier international*, 15–21 April 2010.

8. Francesco Forgione, *'Ndrangheta, boss luoghi e affari della mafia più potente al mondo* ['Ndrangheta, the boss, the locations and the business affairs of the world's most powerful mafia], Milan: Baldini Castoldi Dalai, 2008.

9. "Ndrangheta mafia made more last year than McDonald's and Deutsche Bank', *The Guardian*, 26 March 2014.

10. Antonio Nicaso, 'La nuova Gomorra' [The new Gomorrah], *L'Espresso*, 19 March 2009.

11. Italian Interior Ministry, *Relazione al Parlamento sulle speciale misure di protezione, sulla loro efficacia e sulle modalità generale di applicazione (1° gennaio-30 giugno 2011)* [Report to Parliament on special measures of protection, their effectiveness and their application procedures, 1 January–30 June 2011].

12. Eurispes, op. cit.

13. Antonio Nicaso, *Alle origini della 'Ndrangheta la picciotteria*, Soveria Mannelli: Rubettino, 1993.

14. Grades 9–14 came to light in the course of the July 2010 police operation dubbed 'Il Crimine' or 'Infinite Crime'; see *Ordinanza Crimine del 2010* [operation report], p. 448.

15. Again, this was discovered during the 2010 police operations led jointly by the prefectures of Milan and Reggio di Calabria, which led to the arrest of more than 300 individuals affiliated to the 'Ndrangheta.

16. Delphine Saubaber, 'Découvrir la vérité sur la 'Ndrangheta provoquerait un séisme politique' [Discovering the truth about the 'Ndrangheta would cause a political earthquake], *L'Express*, 20 July 2010.

17. Dessert, op. cit.

18. Archives of Reggio di Calabria, inventory 34, box 59, item 871.

19. Giuseppe Baldessaro, 'Pas de procession, la Mafia sort les flingues' [No procession, the Mafia gets out its guns], *La Repubblica*, published in special edition of *Courrier international*, 15–21 April 2010.

20. 'Calabria, invendita sulle piazze le ballate criminali della 'Ndrangheta' [Calabria, the 'Ndrangheta's criminal ballads on sale in the marketplaces], *Corriere della Sera*, 11 September 1998.

21. Anne Véron, interview with Giuseppe Baldessaro, July 2013.

22. Ibid.

23. Anne Véron, interview with John Dickie, July 2013.

24. Anne Véron, interview with Nicola Gratteri, July 2013.

25. Ibid.

26. Padovani, op. cit.

27. Nicola Gratteri, *La malapianta, conversazione con Antonio Nicaso* [The weed: conversation with Antonio Nicaso], Milan: Mondadori, 2010.

28. Padovani, op. cit.

5. GIUSY PESCE: WIND OF REVOLT

1. Giuseppina Pesce, deposition at the trial of Armeli Signorino, Tribunal of Palmi, 21 May 2012.

2. All Inside, an operation coordinated by the Direzione Investigativa Antimafia of Reggio di Caalbria and jointly carried out by police and *carabinieri*, was launched on 28 April 2010. Two further operations were to follow against the Pesce *cosca*: All Inside 2 (23 November 2010) and All Clean (21 April 2011) which led to the seizure of companies, property and goods worth an estimated €220 million.

3. Francesca Chirico, *Io parlo, donne ribelli in terra di 'Ndrangheta* [I speak out: rebel women in the land of the 'Ndrangheta], Rome: Castelvecchi, 2013.

4. Rosarno's municipal council was twice dissolved due to mafia infiltration, in 1992 and 2008.

5. On 7 January 2010, two African migrants working as seasonal agricultural labourers were wounded with shotguns by young Italians. A riot by several hundred migrant workers followed, condemning the racist attack and protesting against the inhuman conditions in which they lived.

6. According to a 2006 report from the Italian authorities. See Felicity Lawrence, 'Bitter Harvest', *The Guardian*, 19 December 2006.

7. 'World Port Rankings 2011', American Association of Port Authorities (AAPA).

8. Barbara Conforti, 'Mafia, la trahison des femmes' [The Mafia, women betrayed], TV report for *Spécial Investigation*, Canal+ (France), 2 March 2014.

9. Anne Véron, interview with Elisabetta Tripodi, July 2013.

10. Casal di Principe is a *comune* in the province of Caserte, near Naples. It is well known in Italy as the fiefdom of the Casalesi clan, a powerful Camorra group.

11. Michael Day, 'Italy's "eternally unfinished" highway enters final stretch—50 years after construction began', *The Independent*, 19 May 2015.

12. A *comune* in the province of Reggio di Calabria.

13. In his December 2011 depositions at the Tribunal of Palmi during the trial of Armeli Signorino, Marco Ferraro retracted his statement of 2006: 'I don't know, I didn't say or hear anything. It was all her. I said to her: "But Rosa, what are you saying?"'

14. Pesce, op. cit.

15. Giusy's father was considered by his brothers Antonino, Giuseppe, Rocco and Vincenzo as incapable of establishing himself and winning respect, hence his nickname.

16. Lirio Abbate, *Fimmine Ribelli* [Rebel Women], Milan: Rizzoli, 2013.

17. Conforti, op. cit.

18. Ibid.

19. Anne Véron, interview with Alessandra Cerreti, July 2013.

20. Lucio Musolino, ''Ndrangheta, il boss Francesco Pesce arrestato a Rosarno' ['Ndrangheta boss Francesco Pesce arrested in Rosarno], *Il Fatto Quotidiano*, 10 August 2011.

21. Anne Véron, interview with Michele Prestipino, July 2013.

22. 'L'esempio di Giusy Pesce, rivoluzionario' [Giusy Pesce's revolutionary example], *Sole 24 ore*, 11 May 2013.

23. She was still charged with illegal mafia association.

24. Pesce, op. cit.

25. '"All Inside 1 e 2". A Palmi domani al via il processo contro il clan Pesce' ['All Inside 1 and 2'. The trial of the Pesce clan opens tomorrow at Palmi], *Quotidiano della Calabria*, 11 July 2011.

26. Palmi is a *comune* in Reggio di Calabria province.

27. Chirico, op. cit.

28. Rosarno's municipal council was first dissolved in 1992 due to mafia infiltration.

29. The 'All Inside' trial ended in May 2013 with forty convictions, twenty-one acquittals and a combined total sentence of 521 years in prison.

30. Sylvie Veran, 'Mafia, la trahison des femmes' [The Mafia, women betrayed], *Le Nouvel Observateur*, 17 February 2014.

31. Conforti, op. cit.

32. Chirico, op. cit.

6. LEA GAROFALO: THE PRICE OF TREASON

1. Pagliarelle is a neighbourhood in the *comune* of Petilia Policastro.

2. Francesca Chirico, *Io parlo, donne ribelli in terra di 'Ndrangheta* [I speak out: rebel women in the land of the 'Ndrangheta], Rome: Castelvecchi, 2013.

3. Sylvie Veran, 'Mafia, la trahison des femmes' [The Mafia, women betrayed], *Le Nouvel Observateur*, 17 February 2014.

4. Mayor of Milan from 2006 to 2011 for Silvio Berlusconi's Forza Italia party.

5. Prefect of Milan from 2005 to 2013.

6. Marika Demaria, *La scelta di Lea. Lea Garofalo, la ribellione di una donna alla 'Ndrangheta* [Lea's choice: Lea Garofalo, the rebellion of a young woman in the 'Ndrangheta], Milan: Melampo, 2013.

7. Operation Infinite History led to the arrests of Carlo and Giuseppe Cosco as well as Floriano Garofalo.

8. Denise Cosco, deposition at the trial of Carlo Cosco and five others, Tribunal of Milan, July 2011.

9. Milka Kahn, interview with Vicenza Rando, Denise Cosco's lawyer, February 2015.

10. Sylvie Véran, op. cit.

11. The 'Nucleo operativo di protezione' (NOP) is charged with managing the daily lives of justice collaborators and witnesses.

12. Lea Garofalo's letter was published after her death by the *Quotidiano della Calabria*, 2 December 2010.

13. Cosco, op. cit.

14. Libera is Italy's main voluntary anti-mafia organization, founded on 25 March 1995 by Don Luigi Ciotti.

15. Denise and Carmine Venturino began seeing each other in March 2010. The Cosco clan, who had noticed that Denise liked Carmine, had ordered him to seduce her so that they could more easily control her.

16. Cosco, op. cit.
17. *Il Corriere della Sera*, 18 October 2010.
18. Marika Demaria, journalist and editor of the Italian monthly *Narcomafie*, followed the trial and transcribed it on the website Liberainformazione. org.
19. 'Uccisa e sciolta nell'acido, sei ergastoli. Condannato l'ex-compagno' [Killed and dissolved in acid, six life sentences including for ex-partner], *Corriere della Sera*, 30 March 2012.
20. Marika Demaria, 'Carlo Cosco: assumo la responsabilità dell'omicidio di Lea' [Carlo Cosco: 'I take responsibility for Lea Garofalo's murder'], Liberainformazione.org, 9 April 2013.
21. Barbara Conforti, 'Mafia, la trahison des femmes' [The Mafia, women betrayed], TV report for *Spécial Investigation*, Canal+ (France), 2 March 2014.
22. Marika Demaria, 'Processo Garofalo, parla Venturino' [Garofalo trial, Venturino speaks], Liberainformazione.org, April 2013.
23. A *locale* is an entity within the 'Ndrangheta that brings together several families from the same town.
24. Conforti, op. cit.
25. The lowest grade of the 'Ndrangheta's *società maggiore*.
26. Marika Demaria, 'Processo Garofalo: ho ucciso Lea in prede a un raptus' [Garofalo trial, Cosco: 'I killed Lea in a fit of rage'], Liberainformazione.org, 17 April 2013.
27. 'Processo Garofalo: confermato l'ergastolo per Carlo Cosco' [Garofalo trial: life sentence for Carlo Cosco confirmed], Liberaiformazione.org, 29 May 2013.
28. Stefania Prandi, ''Ndrangheta, in un libro, le sofferenze di Lea Garofalo prima di essere uccisa' [The 'Ndrangheta, in a book, the suffering of Lea Garofalo before she was killed], *Il Fatto quotidiano*, 17 October 2013.
29. 'Lea Garofalo, testimone di verità' [Lea Garofalo, witness of truth], Liberainformazione.org, 19 October 2013.
30. Santo Della Volpe, 'Per Lea, per Denise' [For Lea, for Denise], Liberainformazione.org, 21 October 2013.
31. Santo Della Volpe, 'Un coraggio di donne' [Women's courage], Liberainformazione.org, 8 May 2012.

7. THE LAND OF SUICIDES

1. Francesca Chirico, *Io parlo, donne ribelli in terra di 'Ndrangheta* [I speak out, rebel women in the land of the 'Ndrangheta], Rome: Castelvecchi, 2013.

2. Giuseppe Creazzo and deputy public prosecutor Giulia Masci.

3. The Bellocco clan, along with their Pesce counterparts, are one of the 'Ndrangheta's most powerful families in Rosarno. Gregorio Bellocco married the sister of Michele Cacciola and aunt of Maria Concetta, Teresa Cacciola.

4. Lirio Abbate, *Fimmine Ribelli* [Rebel Women], Milan: Rizzoli, 2013.

5. Operation Wild Wood (*Bosco selvaggio*), conducted in November 2005 by the Direzione Distrettuale Antimafia in Reggio di Calabria, led to the arrest of Gregorio Bellocco and some twenty affiliates of his clan.

6. Francesca Viscone, *La globalizzazione delle cattive idee: Mafia, musica, mass media* [The globalization of bad ideas: Mafia, music, mass media], Soveria Manelli: Rubbettino, 2005.

7. A small *comune* in the province of Cosenza, Calabria.

8. Francesca Chirico, 'Gole bruciate' [Burnt throats], special edition 'Donne di 'Ndrangheta' [Women of the 'Ndrangheta], *Narcomafie*, March 2012.

9. Michele Prestipino, 'Frammenti per una riflessione sul caso calabrese' [Fragments for reflection on the Calabrian case], *Narcomafie*, March 2012.

10. Alessandra Dino, 'Un mondo in frantumi' [A world in pieces], *Narcomafie*, March 2012.

11. Lucio Musolino, 'Se il boss denuncia lo Stato' [If the boss accuses the state], *Corriere della Calabria*, 14 August 2011.

12. Lucio Musolino, 'Quella strana morte in casa Mancuso' [That strange death in the Mancuso household], *Corriere della Calabria*, 6 August 2011.

13. Anne Véron, interview with Michele Prestipino, July 2013.

PART THREE: WOMEN IN THE CAMORRA

1. English-language edition: Roberto Saviano, *Gomorrah: Italy's Other Mafia*, London: Pan Macmillan, 2011.

2. Jean-Jacques Bozonnet, 'La Camorra: Naples sous l'empire du crime [The Camorra: Naples under the rule of crime], *Le Monde*, 10 November 2006.

3. Saviano, op. cit.

4. Anne Véron, interview with Isaia Sales, March 2015.

5. Ibid.

6. Ibid.

7. A Neapolitan term (singular *guappo*) derived from the Spanish word *guapo*, originally meaning 'ruffian' but later meaning 'handsome man' or 'dandy'.

8. Véron, interview with Isaia Sales, op. cit.

9. Matilde Serao, *Il paese di Cuccagna*, Milan: Treves, 1891 [English translation: *The Land of Cockayne*, London: Heinemann, 1901].

10. Isaia Sales, 'Donne di Camorra' [Women of the Camorra], lecture at Suor Orsola Benincasa University, Naples, 2014.

11. Véron, interview with Isaia Sales, op. cit.

12. According to certain sources, US intelligence asked Luciano to re-establish contact with Sicilian mafia families in 1943, the godfather of Palermo in particular, so that they could assist the Allied landing in Sicily. The mafia played a significant part in the success of the military operation—something Luciano denied in his 'Last Testament'.

13. Carlo Lucarelli, *Blu Notte. La Storia della Camorra* [Midnight Blue: The Story of the Camorra], RAI documentary, 2011.

14. Véron, interview with Isaia Sales, op. cit.

15. Giuseppe Marrazzo, *Il Camorrista*, Naples: Tullio Pironti, 1984. A film of the same name, directed by Giuseppe Tornatore, was inspired by Marrazzo's book.

16. Véron, interview with Isaia Sales, op. cit.

17. Anne Véron, interview with Rosaria Capacchione, March 2015.

18. Véron, interview with Isaia Sales, op. cit.

19. Camorra Observatory, an anti-mafia association founded in 1981.

20. Salvatore Aloïse, 'Après le séisme des Abruzzes, l'Italie cherche à éviter une emprise de la Mafia sur la reconstruction' [After the Abruzzo earthquake, Italy tries to prevent a mafia takeover in construction], *Le Monde*, 8 May 2009.

21. 'Ordures ou richesses: les poubelles du monde' [Rubbish or riches: the world's dustbins], *CultureMonde*, radio programme, France Culture, 12 November 2012.

22. Interview with Rosaria Capacchione, *op. cit.*

23. Anna Maria Zaccaria, 'Donne di Camorra' [Women of the Camorra], in Gabriella Gribaudi, *Traffici criminali, Camorra, mafie e reti internazionali dell'illegalità*, Turin: Bollati Boringhieri, 2009.

24. Véron, interview with Isaia Sales, op. cit.

25. Not her real name.

26. Véron, interview with Rosaria Capacchione, op. cit.

27. Anne Véron, interview with Gabriella Gribaudi, April 2014.

28. *La Repubblica*, 12 February 2014.

29. *La Repubblica*, 12 February 2009.

8. PUPETTA MARESCA: INSULTED HONOUR

1. Clare Longrigg, *Mafia Women*, London: Chatto & Windus, 1997.

2. Hans Magnus Enzensberger, 'Pupetta Maresca, L'angelo del crimine che sparo per amore' [Pupetta Maresca, the angel of crime who shot for love], *La Repubblica*, 15 August 1998.

3. Anne Véron, interview with Isaia Sales, March 2015.

4. Giovanni Fiandaca (ed.), *Women and the Mafia: Female Roles in Organized Crime Structures*, New York: Springer, 2007.

5. Padre Pio, whose real name was Francesco Forgione, was born in Pietrelcina (Campania) in 1887 and died in 1968 at San Giovanni Rotondo (Puglia). He was a Capuchin monk and priest, venerated in the south of Italy after he reported bearing the stigmata of Christ's crucifixion. He was canonized by Pope John Paul II in 2002.

6. Fiandaca, op. cit.

7. Véron, interview with Isaia Sales, op. cit.

8. Longrigg, op. cit.

9. Ibid.

10. 'La Legge d'Onore', *Time Magazine*, 20 April 1959; 'Crimes of Honor Debated by Italy; Trial of Woman in Naples for Murder of Husband's Rival Stirs Nation', *The New York Times*, 7 April 1959.

11. *Roma*, 2 April 1959.

12. Anne Véron, interview with 'Maria', February 2015.

13. Longrigg, op. cit.

14. Giorgio Dell'Arti, 'Pupetta Maresca', *Cinquantamila*, *Corriere della Sera* online, http://www.cinquantamila.it/storyTellerThread.php?threadId=MARESCA+Pupetta (last accessed 2 December 2016).

15. Longrigg, op. cit.

16. Anne Véron, interview with Rosaria Capacchione, March 2015.

17. Ermanno Corsi, 'Carcere a luci rosse, la direttrice a giudizio' [Red light prison: the director to be judged], *La Repubblica*, 18 March 1989.

18. Franco Coppola, 'Cutolo, Cirillo, Sismi Il "Giallo" Semerari è un intrigo di Stato' [Cutolo, Cirillo, SISMI and the Semerari 'whodunnit' are a state intrigue], *La Repubblica*, 21 May 1985.

19. Longrigg, op. cit.

20. 'Casa di Pupetta Maresca diventa sede di volontariato' [Pupetta Maresca's home becomes charity work HQ], *La Repubblica*, 26 February 2004.

21. Longrigg, op. cit.

22. Enzo D'Errico, interview with Pupetta Maresca, *Corriere della Sera*, 2 July 1994.

23. Longrigg, op. cit.

9. ERMINIA GIULIANO: 'LADY CAMORRA'

1. Marcelle Padovani, *Mafia, mafias*, Paris: Gallimard, 2009.

2. Anne Véron, interview with Giuseppe Narducci, March 2015.

3. Ibid.

4. Anne Véron, interview with Rosaria Capacchione, March 2015.

5. Anna Maria Zaccaria, 'L'emergenza rosa. Dati e suggestioni sulle donne di camorra' [The pink peril: Facts and hypotheses on the Camorra's women], *Meridiana. Rivista di storia e scienze sociali*, no. 67: *Donne di mafia*, 2010.

6. Tribunal of Naples, 7th criminal section, trial no. 4426/06 of the Giuliano clan.

7. Zaccaria, op. cit.

8. Vincenzo Vincenzo, 'Arrestata lady Camorra, devo pettinarmi' [Lady Camorra arrested: I need to have my hair done], *Corriere della Sera*, 24 December 2000.

9. Dario Del Porto, 'Dieci anni per Celeste Giuliano, condannata come un capoclan' [Ten years in jail for Celeste Giuliano, sentenced as a clan *capo*], *La Repubblica*, 20 April 2006.

10. Giorgio Dell'Arti, 'Erminia Giuliano', *Corriere della Sera* online, 7 May 2014.

10. MARIA LICCIARDI: 'THE GODMOTHER'

1. Henri Haget, 'La marraine de Naples' [The Godmother of Naples], *L'Express*, 13 August 2009.

2. Giorgio Dell'Arti, 'Maria Licciardi', *Cinquantamila*, *Corriere della Sera* online, http://www.cinquantamila.it/storyTellerThread.php?threadId= LICCIARDI+Maria (last accessed 2 December 2016).

3. Flaminia Giambalvo, 'Barbara Sargenti: storia di una PM che non molla' [Barbara Sargenti: the story of a prosecutor who doesn't let go], *D'attualità*, weekly magazine of *La Repubblica*, 20 May 2014.

4. Matthew Carney, 'Mafia Mamma' SBS, 14 February 2001, http://www. sbs.com.au/news/article/2001/02/14/mafia-mamma (last accessed 2 December 2016).

5. Ibid.

6. Giovanni Fiandaca (ed.), *Women and the Mafia: Female Roles in Organized Crime Structures*, New York: Springer, 2007.

7. Rory Carroll, 'Italy's most wanted Mamma', *The Guardian*, 30 June 2000.

8. 'Arrestata Maria Licciardi, capoclan di Secondigliano' [Maria Licciardi, chief of the Secondigliano clan, arrested], *La Repubblica*, 15 June 2001.

9. Zaccaria, op. cit.

11. GIUSEPPINA NAPPA: FAITHFUL TO 'SANDOKAN'

1. Dominique Dunglas, 'L'extraordinaire planque du parrain de la Camorra' [The extraordinary hideout of the Camorra godfather], *Le Parisien*, 13 July 1998. Roberto Saviano estimated the net worth of the Schiavone family in 2008 at US$47 billion. See Roberto Saviano, 'Striking Back Against the Mob', *The Washington Post*, 29 June 2008.

2. Dunglas, op. cit.

3. Ibid.

4. There is a NATO base near Casal di Principe.

5. Anne Véron, interview with Rosaria Capacchione, March 2015.

6. 'L'omelia non è piaciuta alla moglie di Sandokan' [Sandokan's wife disapproved of homily], *Il mattino*, 30 October 2011.

12. ANNA CARRINO: THE WOMAN WHO SCARED THE CASALESI CLAN

1. Flaminia Giambalvo, 'Anna Carrino, pentita per gelosia' [Anna Carrino, informer out of jealousy], *D'attualità*, weekly magazine of *La Repubblica*, 27 November 2014.

2. The Casalesi are the principal clan within the Neapolitan Camorra. Their fiefdom is in Casal di Principe, in the province of Caserte, Campania (the region of Naples).

3. Anne Véron, interview with Rosaria Capacchione, March 2015.

4. Francesco Bidognetti was born in 1951, Anna Carrino in 1966.

5. 'Collabora la moglie del boss Francesco Bidognetti e fa arrestare anche il figlio' [The wife of boss Francesco Bidognetti collaborates and has his son arrested], *Corriere del Mezzogiorno*, 17 April 2008.

6. Roberto Saviano, 'Quando il camorrista uccide per nulla' [When the *camorrista* kills for nothing], *La Repubblica*, 8 October 2012.

7. Giambalvo, op. cit.

8. Roberto Saviano, 'Il matriarcato' [The matriarchy], *Corriere della Sera*, 16 April 2005.

9. Giambalvo, op. cit.

10. Ibid.

11. Antonio Corbo, 'Casalesi, parla la donna del clan' [Casalesi, the woman of the clan tells all], *La Repubblica*, 20 November 2007.

12. Fulvio Bufi, 'Parla la donna del boss Retata tra i Casalesi' [The boss' wife accuses: round-up of the Casalesi clan], *Corriere della Sera*, 18 April 2008.

13. 'Arrestato Gianluca Bidognetti, tentò di uccidere la zia e la cugina' [Gianluca Bidognetti arrested, attempted to kill his aunt and cousin], *La Repubblica*, 21 November 2008.

14. 'Casalesi, sventato un attentato contro la superpentita Anna Carrino, ex-compagna del boss Bidognetti' [Casalesi clan: a foiled attack against

the *superpentita* Anna Carrino, ex-companion of boss Bidognetti], *Il Mattino*, 15 February 2011.

15. Giambalvo, op. cit.

INDEX

INDEX

INDEX

INDEX

INDEX

INDEX

INDEX

INDEX

INDEX

INDEX

INDEX

INDEX